T0171702

MEETING
GOD
on the
MOUNTAIN

Verla M. Blom

WESTBOW
PRESS®
A DIVISION OF THOMAS NELSON
& ZONDERVAN

WestBow Press books may be ordered through booksellers or by contacting:

WestBow Press
A Division of Thomas Nelson & Zondervan
1663 Liberty Drive
Bloomington, IN 47403
www.westbowpress.com
1 (866) 928-1240

ISBN: 978-1-5127-2927-6 (sc)
ISBN: 978-1-5127-2926-9 (e)

Library of Congress Control Number: 2016901532

Print information available on the last page.

WestBow Press rev. date: 2/19/2016

Contents

Acknowledgements

Deep gratitude to:

My God of the mountains: Who invites me to remember that all of my help comes from Him.

My husband Jerry: who encouraged me to pick up my pen when I put down my stethoscope. During his own treatment for cancer, Jerry taught me that "being" is more important than "doing." He captured many of this book's photographic images during our mountain adventures in Montana and Wyoming. In addition to being my fellow traveler, Jerry continues to be my teacher, tech support, provider of commentaries and pastor.

Dawn Michelson (West Africa): who taught me, through her writing, that one can travel to distant places via the words of someone who has been there.

Bozeman Christian Reformed Church (Montana): who gave us the opportunity to move to Mountain Country and who provided many friends and experienced hikers. Special acknowledgement to Frank and Linda James and Carl and Kathy Wierda who offered friendly editing of these lessons during our Adult Sunday School Class which was entitled, "Mountain Devotions." Also "Hurrahs" to my fellow hiker, Judy Kingma, who stopped without complaint whenever she heard "Photo!"

Dorothy and Daryl Baar (South Dakota) and Joann Vogel (Michigan): who pray and encourage as only heart-friends can.

Barb Vogel (Minnesota): who read the chapters, made editorial notations and gave the final push toward publication.

Guests around our dining room table: who inspire me with how they meet God on the mountains. Naming all these family members and friends would require a book itself; but special thanks go to my brother, Byron Hoogwerf, with whom I have shared both mountains and valleys. The best mountain hikes and conversations have been with our three knowledgeable sons (Eliot, Nathan and Travis), their gracious wives (Sue, Amy and Beckie) and the nine most beautiful grandchildren in the world (Alyssa, Lexi, Jackson, Carson, Ian, Trevor, Henry, Tobin and Rahlee). My prayer is that each of you continues to meet God wherever you live!

Introduction

"Come, let us go up to the mountain of the Lord . . . He will teach us His ways, so that we may walk in His paths."
— Micah 4:2

Meet Bible characters who walked mountain paths with God.

Learn about the God of the mountains.

Use the questions at the end of each chapter for personal reflection or as a stimulus for group discussion.

Come and mountain climb!

As the mountains surround Jerusalem, so the Lord surrounds his people both now and forevermore.

—Psalm 125:2

Chapter One

God of the Mountains

As the mountains surround Jerusalem, so the Lord surrounds
his people both now and forevermore.

—Psalm 125:2

After growing up near the flat plains of Minnesota and then living near the sparkling lakes of Michigan, my husband and I moved to the mountain country of Montana. Psalm 125 became our theme as we faced the uncertainty of each day. Psalm 125:1 assured us of God's protection especially during the unsettling transitions following our move. *"Those who trust in the Lord are like Mt. Zion, which cannot be shaken, but endures forever."* However, we modified Psalm 125:2 to become,

> *"As the mountains surround Bozeman, so the Lord surrounds*
> *Jerry and Verla both now and forevermore."*

Bozeman, Montana, located in the Gallatin Valley, is surrounded by Rocky Mountain Ranges. Many hiking trails in this area provide spectacular views of these 8,000 to 10,000 feet elevations. Some of these trails have enticing names like Sundance Trail and Painted Hills Trail. The title "Peets Hill" sounds nondescript for a hiking trail on the eastern edge of downtown Bozeman. However, after a short ascent up this hill, one can view the Bridger Mountains to the north, the Gallatin Range to the southeast, the Madison Range to the southwest and the Tobacco Root Mountains to the west. As I stand on Peets Hill during winter beauty and during springtime splendor, I gaze with awe at the surrounding foothills and mountain peaks. I ask myself, "Who is this God of mine who surrounds me just as these indescribable mountains surround Bozeman?"

Psalm 90 verses 1 and 2 give me insight into this God of the mountains.

> *Lord, you have been our dwelling place throughout all the generations. Before the mountains were born or you brought forth the earth and the world, from everlasting to everlasting, you are God.*

My God of the mountains is God from everlasting to everlasting. My God of the mountains was God before even the formation of mountains. My God of the mountains has no beginning and no end. Sometimes as I scan mountain ranges, I cannot see a beginning or an end. However, when I look on a map, I see that the mountain terrain stops. The mountainous landscape does not stretch from Montana to Minnesota and on to Michigan. In contrast, my God of the mountains is from everlasting to everlasting. His history has no beginning. His story has no end. I cannot fathom this eternal nature of God, but Psalm 90 says He is from everlasting to everlasting, so I believe what I cannot understand.

Psalm 65:5 and 6 tell me something else about my everlasting God of the mountains. *"You answer us with awesome deeds of righteousness, O God . . . who formed the mountains by your power."*

My everlasting God of the mountains formed the mountains by His power. I cannot fathom this creativity. I cannot fathom this power. But Psalm 65 says God formed the mountains by His creative power; so I believe what I cannot understand.

Majestic is a word that is often used to describe the snow-capped peak of Lone Mountain in Big Sky country. Majestic implies something that is lofty, regal and grand. Psalm 76:4 describes God with the words, *"You are resplendent with light, more majestic than mountains rich with game."* This Psalm tells me that my everlasting God of the mountains is even more majestic than the mountains that He formed by his power. When the sun rises or sets over the mountains, the brilliant rays make the angles of the slopes resplendent in their majesty. God is even more resplendent! I cannot understand God's majesty or His resplendence, but I believe what I cannot understand.

As I reflect on this God of the mountain, I don't understand how He can surround me. I don't understand His eternal nature. I don't understand His creativity and power. I don't understand His might and resplendence. However, I believe what I cannot understand and I respond with Psalm 104:

> *Praise the Lord, O my soul. O Lord, my God, you are very great; You are clothed with splendor and majesty. May the glory of the Lord endure forever; may the LORD rejoice in his works---he who looks at the earth and it trembles, who touches the mountains, and they smoke. I will sing to the Lord all my life; I will sing praise to my God as long as l live.*

Reflections: Read Psalm 125 and Psalm 104

1. What do these Psalms tell you about mountains?

2. What do these Psalms tell you about the God of the mountains?

3. What is your response?

The waters rose and covered the mountains to a depth of more than twenty feet.

—Genesis 7:20

Chapter Two

Mountain Man Noah

The waters rose and covered the mountains to a depth of more than twenty feet.

—Genesis 7:20

The Yellowstone River, Gallatin River, Jefferson River and the Madison River occasionally flood their banks as the mountain snow melts during the spring of the year. Sometimes, creeks in Montana also flow rapidly during late May and early June. Printed instructions for hikers often indicate that one can "stone hop" across a creek bed. However, crossing a creek on foot during "flood stage" is not safe. During my springtime hikes in Montana, I have had to detour from my planned route due to deep water in creek beds.

Noah had a deep water detour in his life, too, when God said to him,

> *I am going to put an end to all people, for the earth is filled with violence because of them. I am surely going to destroy both them and the earth. So make yourself an ark of cypress wood. . . .*
>
> —Genesis 6:13-14a

When we read about the flood story in Genesis chapters 6-9, we often focus on the building of the ark, the animals marching two by two, the flood itself or even the rainbow with its beautiful significance. Since living in mountain country, I have gained a new perspective on this Genesis account. I have begun to think of Noah as a mountain man with a deep water detour.

After Mountain Man Noah, his family and the animals had entered the ark and after God had shut them in, Mountain Man Noah felt the tilt of the ark and experienced the reality of: *"as the waters increased they lifted the ark high above the earth"* (Genesis 7:17). Mountain Man Noah was secluded in the ark when *"the waters rose and covered the mountains to a depth of more than twenty feet"* (Genesis 7:20). Mountain Man Noah likely felt either a lurch or a gentle nestling of the ark as *"on the seventeenth day of the seventh month the ark came to rest on the mountains of Ararat"* (Genesis 8:4). Mount Ararat is considered to be the highest elevation in this mountain range located in Eastern Turkey. When I gaze at mountain ranges in Southwestern Montana, I try to picture how an ark could come to "rest on the mountain." Only the God of the mountains could send a flood. Only the God of the mountains could protect Noah in an ark during that flood. Only the God of the mountains could settle that ark on those mountains with Noah inside as the flood waters began to recede.

Genesis 8:6 tells us that Noah opened the window of the ark to send out a raven when he wanted to assess how much the flood waters had gone down. I wonder how many other times Noah opened the window of the ark. Genesis chapter 8 also tells us that it was almost two and a half months after the ark rested on the mountains of Ararat before *"the tops of the mountains became visible"* (Genesis 8:5).

Did Noah look out of that same window of the ark to peer at the tops of the mountains as they gradually became visible? Mountain Man Noah no doubt was intrigued by those newly washed mountain peaks as the flood waters receded. As he waited to celebrate his 601st birthday, did Noah recognize the rebirth of the earth as well as the implications of his own remarkable incubation in the womb of the ark?

Genesis does not tell us what Noah felt during his many months in the ark. However, Genesis does tell us that Noah listened to the voice of God.

When God told Noah to build an ark; Noah built an ark. When God told Noah to go in the ark; Noah went into the ark. When God told Noah to come out of the ark; Noah came out of the ark. We don't know how long it took Noah, his family and the animals to come out of the ark. However, because the ark had rested on the mountains of Ararat, they must have had a significant descent ahead of them. We do know that after the waters of the flood had completely receded, Mountain Man Noah built an altar to the Lord and the aroma of Noah's sacrifice was pleasing to God.

Noah's mountain top experience is unlike anything we will have to encounter. However, Noah's God is still a God who speaks to us. Noah's God is still a God who gives us a place to rest. Noah's God is still a God who finds the sacrifice that Jesus made for our sins is a pleasing aroma whether we acknowledge that sacrifice while on a mountain top, during a descent or in a valley. The Genesis account of Mountain Man Noah gives us some insights in to the life of Noah. This account also gives us insight into the ways that God speaks, acts, protects and preserves. Finally, this account gives us wonderful insight into the ways that God prepares His people for Eternal Life with Him.

Reflections: Read Genesis 7:17 through 8:22

1. How would you feel if you were confined in an ark for over a year?

2. What destruction is described in Genesis 7:17 through 8:22?

3. What evidence of redemption is displayed in Genesis 7:17 through 8:22?

4. Describe Noah's response to his situation after the flood waters began to recede.

5. Describe Noah's response to God after he and his family left the ark.

6. What is your own response to this mountain story?

So Abraham called that place The LORD Will Provide. And to this day it is said, "On the mountain of the LORD it will be provided."

—Genesis 22:14

Chapter Three

Mountain Man Abraham

So Abraham called that place The LORD Will Provide. And to this day it is said, "On the mountain of the LORD it will be provided."

—Genesis 22:14

The Biblical account of Abraham taking Isaac up Mount Moriah is a story that describes not only attributes of Abraham and Isaac, but this narrative also reveals names and attributes of God. I like to meditate on the names of God while I am hiking mountain trails. As I am exercising physically, I also exercise mentally and spiritually by silently listing God's names and/ or attributes alphabetically. For example, God is Adonai, Bread of Life, Creator, Deliverer, Everlasting, Father, Great, Healer, Infinite, Just, Kind, Loving, Mighty, Name above all names, Omnipresent, Powerful, Quieter of my soul, Righteous, Savior, Trustworthy, Unchangeable, Victorious, Wise, Exalted, Yahweh, Zealous.

Abraham and Isaac had three days to hike before they reached the place that God told them was their destination. I wonder if they meditated on and talked about the attributes of God as they walked and waited. Abraham knew God as "The LORD" who spoke to him when his name was still Abram. Genesis 12 recounts God's promises to Abram that God would make him into a great nation; God would bless him; God would make his name great; and God promised that all the nations on earth would be blessed through him. As the LORD made those promises, He told Abram, *"Go to the land I will* show you" (Genesis 12:1). Now years later, Abraham again heard God say, *"Go to one of the mountains I will tell you about"* (Genesis 22:2).

Abram, at age 75, willingly obeyed when he first heard God's voice saying, "Go!" In response to that first calling, Abram traveled from Haran to Shechem. The LORD appeared to him there and promised, *"To your offspring I will give this land"* (Genesis 12:7). Abram built an altar to the LORD at Shechem. From there, Abram traveled to the hills east of Bethel where Abram again built an altar to the LORD. In fact, traveling from place to place and building altars was an integral part of Abram's life. Abram knew His God as a God worthy of worship!

So, now as Abraham and Isaac are hiking, I can imagine Abraham telling Isaac the stories of his early travels. Abraham could be recalling that his God is not only a God who is worthy of worship, but He is also a God who keeps His promises. Abram, at age 99, had heard God's voice saying, *"I will confirm my covenant between me and you and will greatly increase your numbers"* (Genesis 17:2). God changed Abram's name to Abraham and promised to make him a father of many nations through his yet-to-be born son Isaac. No doubt Isaac had often heard of his unusual birth and the covenant promises that would be kept through him and his future children. I can picture Abraham and Isaac recalling these past promises which had come from the voice of God.

Abraham and Isaac knew God as one who is worthy of worship, as one who keeps His promises, but also as a God who is to be obeyed.

Both Abraham and Isaac willingly obeyed God in starting their three day walk to Mount Moriah. Abraham had heard God's voice, *"Take your son, your only son, Isaac, whom you love. . . sacrifice him. . ."* (Genesis 22:2). In obedience, Isaac carried the wood for the sacrifice. In obedience, Abraham carried the fire and the knife. They listened to God's voice when *"they reached the place God told him about"* (Genesis 22:9). In obedience and faith, Abraham built an altar. In obedience and faith, Abraham bound his only son—his covenantal son—and laid him on the altar on top of the wood. In obedience and faith, Abraham reached out his hand and holding the knife was ready to slay his son. In promise-keeping intervention, God stopped Abraham and provided a ram for the burnt offering to take the place of Isaac. At that substitutionary moment, Abraham and Isaac learned another name for their worship-worthy, promise-keeping, obedience-demanding God. Abraham proclaimed "Jehovah Jireh" which means the LORD will provide or the LORD will see to it. God provided a sacrifice and "saw to it" that Isaac lived. After God once again renewed His covenant promises, Abraham and Isaac's journey down Mount Moriah was probably filled with conversation and meditation about worship, covenant renewal, obedience rewarded and timely provisions.

This Abraham and Isaac story foreshadowed the fact that one day God, the Father, would take His Son, His only Son, whom He loved, to that same region of Moriah near Jerusalem and sacrifice Him there for the salvation of those who believe that God has provided. God has seen to it. Jehovah Jireh. The LORD Will Provide for now and always.

Reflections: Read Genesis 22:1-19

1. How was Abraham tested?

2. How did Abraham demonstrate his faith?

3. Of what significance is the phrase "On the mountain of the LORD it will be provided"?

4. How have you been tested and what has been your response?

5. What name or attribute of God is the most meaningful to you?

"You yourselves have seen what I did to Egypt, and how I carried you on eagles' wings and brought you to myself."
—Exodus 19:4

Chapter Four

Mountain Man Moses

*The Lord descended to the top of Mount Sinai and called
Moses to the top of the mountain. So Moses went up.*
                                                    —Exodus 19:20

In the early 1800's fur trappers roamed the area which is now known as
the state of Montana. These independent souls, such as Jedediah Smith
and John Coulter, were known as mountain men. As I hike well-marked
trails, I try to picture what life was like for these frontiersmen.

Sourdough Canyon Road is one of the well-marked trails near Bozeman.
On a springtime hike, I discovered elk fur on the trail and could see
where a predator had dragged a carcass down to Sourdough Creek. I
could imagine the sounds of that encounter. Jedediah Smith and John
Coulter, rugged mountain men, would likely have heard sounds and seen
sights that were new to their ears and eyes. The mountains and canyons
of Montana were a wilderness of new adventure for these travelers in the
early nineteenth century.

As I hiked Sourdough Canyon Road, I thought of a mountain man who
lived even before the mountain men of Montana. Moses was a mountain
man who did a lot of hiking, too. I do not know how he found the top of
Mount Sinai, but I know that he had the God of the mountains as his Trail
Guide. Exodus 19:3 tells us, *"Then Moses went up to God and the LORD
called to him from the mountain. . . ."* As I hike in the mountains and curve

around the switchbacks, I wonder if Moses took a zigzag path or if he went straight up to the top of Mount Sinai. I do know that within the narrative of Exodus 19, Moses went up and down the mountain at least three times. He went up to God; he went down to the people.

As a mountain man, Moses was likely well acquainted with the sounds and sights of nature. Exodus 19 tells us about some of the mountain wildlife that he probably saw. As Moses went up to God, he heard God say, *"You yourselves have seen what I did to Egypt, and how I carried you on eagles' wings and brought you to myself"* (Exodus 19:4). That word picture was no doubt vivid to Moses since the regal eagle was a bird of the mountains. Moses possibly also saw mountain rams whose horns could have been used as trumpets. God warned Moses that the people who were in his charge were not to go up the mountain until they heard the ram's horn sound a long blast (Exodus 19:13b).

However, Moses' most important role was not to observe nature. Moses' most important role was not to plot new trails up and down Mt. Sinai. Moses' most important role was to represent God to the children of Israel and to represent the Israelites to God. Moses, as a mountain man, experienced the sounds and sights of God Himself.

Exodus 19:16-19 describe some of those sights and sounds: thunder, lightening, thick cloud, loud trumpet blast, Mt. Sinai covered with smoke, and the whole mountain trembling violently. The most vivid sight was God's Presence, *"Mount Sinai was covered with smoke, because the LORD descended on it with fire"* (verse 18). The most vivid sound was the voice of God. *"Then Moses spoke and the voice of God answered him"* (verse 19).

God had commanded Moses to put limits for the people around the mountain. God's holiness demanded that only a mediator could approach His deity. The Israelites needed someone as a go-between. God appointed Moses as that person. In Exodus 19, we read about Moses going up to God; God calling to him from the mountain and telling him, *"This is what you are to tell the people of Israel."* In Exodus 18:15, Moses explains, *"the people come to me to explain God's will."* This shows us that God spoke to Moses and Moses, in turn, spoke God's word to the people. In addition, Exodus 19:8 tells us, "The *people all responded together, 'We will do everything the LORD has said.' So Moses brought their answer back to God."*

Moses was a mediator mountain man. One of his mountain top experiences where he saw the Glory of God and where he heard God's voice lasted 40 days and 40 nights (Exodus 24). However, Moses was not a perfect mountain man. Just as Jedediah Smith and John Coulter prepared the way for other mountain people, Moses prepared the way for the Perfect Mediator, Jesus. Only Jesus Himself, both God and man, could be a mediator between the Holy God of the mountains and his imperfect desert dwellers. Jesus experienced the sights and sounds of heaven to bring God's Word to us. Jesus experienced the sights and sounds of earth to bring our words to God.

May we stand in awe just as the children of Israel did:

> *When the people saw the thunder and lightening and heard the trumpet and saw the mountain in smoke, they trembled with fear.*
>
> —Exodus 20:18

Reflections: Read Exodus 19

1. What sights and sounds have you experienced on mountains or in nature?

2. What strikes you about Moses going back and forth between the people and God?

3. Why do we no longer need a man like Moses to be a mediator between God and us?

4. What have you learned from studying Exodus 19?

5. What difference will it make in how you live tomorrow?

And Aaron died there on top of the mountain.
—Numbers 20:28b

Chapter Five

Mountain Man Aaron

And Aaron died there on top of the mountain.
—Numbers 20:28b

Deaths related to mountain mishaps are reported almost monthly in Montana newspapers. Skiers get caught in avalanches and die. Rock climbers slip from their footholds and die. Hikers misjudge their surroundings and die. These deaths on rugged mountains are generally unplanned and tragic.

Aaron's death on Mount Hor was different. God clearly told Moses and Aaron that Aaron would die on the top of a mountain. As this one hundred twenty three year old man trekked up the mountain, Aaron's hike was observed by the Israelite community who were camped at the base of Mount Hor near the border of Edom. When we observe hikers today, we often see them assisted by walking sticks or climbing poles. When we observe hikers today, we see them wearing synthetic hiking clothes and transporting heavy backpacks. We do not know if the children of Israel were able to see Aaron carry his staff as a walking stick. We could assume that Aaron was wearing at least a portion of his priestly garments which had been made by his people. These robes of gold, blue, purple and scarlet are described for us in Exodus 28. The tunic of fine linen, the carefully crafted ephod, the symbolic breastpiece, the pomegranates and gold bells, the embroidered sash and dignified turban were astonishing mountain gear. Aaron, while wearing his sacred garments, had interceded for these people as their priest in route from Egypt to this stopover. Now priest-clad

Aaron, stately Moses, and Aaron's son, Eleazar, ascended Mount Hor in full awareness that Aaron would die there.

God had told Aaron that he would not enter the land of Canaan because he had rebelled against God at the waters of Meribah. However, this story of Aaron ascending to his death does not have a tragic tone. God's tenderness is affirmed in phrases like, *"Aaron will be gathered to his people"* (Numbers 20:24a) and *"Remove Aaron's garments and put them on his son, Eleazar"* (Numbers 20:26a). Aaron knew the promise that he was part of a kingdom of priests. He knew from that promise that Eleazar would carry on the priesthood.

So as I picture Moses, Aaron and Eleazar obeying their God of the mountains, I hear the gold bells on the hem of Aaron's garments. I sense the peace of God's presence and the grandeur of God's holiness. After years of wandering in the wilderness, Aaron is promised eternal rest. On the top of the mountain, Moses removes Aaron's garments and places them on Eleazar. Aaron exchanges his colorful, but possibly dusty, mountain robe for a bright, glorious, and heavenly white robe. When I read, *"and Aaron died there on top of the mountain,"* I don't have the sense of a tragic death. I sense a death that was planned and orchestrated by our God of justice, compassion and perfect Sovereignty.

I have never seen Mount Hor. I have never camped at the base of that elevation. However, I have seen and climbed to mountain peaks in Montana. I have felt the presence of God in marvelous ways on those mountain tops. I have thought that Aaron was blessed to make his final climb accompanied by his brother, Moses and his son, Eleazar. I have thought that Aaron was blessed to be able to die on the top of a mountain and be cradled there in the arms of God. Even more, I rejoice in the blessing that because Jesus became my Great High Priest, I will someday wear Robes of Righteousness just like Aaron.

Reflections: Read Numbers 20:1-13 and 22-29.

1. Why did God tell Moses and Aaron that they would not be able to enter the Land of Canaan?

2. How do you feel about this decision by God?

3. What impresses you about Aaron's hike up Mount Hor?

4. What was the response of the Israelites to Aaron's death?

5. What is your response to the death of someone you love?

6. What does it mean to you that Jesus is a High Priest Who is greater than Aaron? (see Hebrews 4:14-16)

Then Joshua built on Mount Ebal an altar to the LORD, the God of Israel.

—Joshua 8:30

Chapter Six

Mountain Man Joshua

Then Joshua built on Mount Ebal an altar to the LORD, the God of Israel.

—Joshua 8:30

Joshua 8 tells the story of Joshua building an altar using stones which had not been touched by any iron tool. The Bible does not tell us how big this altar was or how big the stones were that Joshua used. The Bible does tell us that this mountain event was significant in the life of the Israelites.

When my granddaughter and I climbed on the east side of the Bridger Mountains, we struggled over rocky paths before we came to a pile of stones known as a cairn. This cairn or monument is the marker where one trail goes south to Sacagawea Peak and another trail leads north to Hardscrabble Peak. When I looked at that pile of stones on the mountain trail, I did not immediately think of an altar. I did realize that this monument was a significant marker or guide indicating which path to take in order to reach Sacagawea Peak.

Mountain man Joshua also knew that he had to have a Guide in order to follow the right path. Joshua had been an apprentice of Moses who was the first leader of the children of Israel as they exited Egypt and journeyed to the Promised Land of Canaan. Joshua had heard the words of Moses which are recorded in Deuteronomy 27. God, through Moses, gave instructions about what the Israelites were to do after they had crossed the Jordan River and entered the Promised Land. God commanded the people to set up large stones at Mount Ebal and build an altar there. God told them to offer burnt offerings, sacrifice fellowship offerings, and rejoice in the presence of the Lord. The people were also commanded to write the law clearly on plaster-coated stones.

Moses was now dead. Joshua was the leader of the Israelites. Joshua knew that in order to lead them on the right path, he needed to listen to God, his Guide. Mountain man Joshua did just that. He listened and he obeyed. Joshua chapter 8 tells us that leader Joshua gathered uncut stones and built an altar on Mount Ebal just as God had commanded. Burnt offerings were offered on that altar to represent the need for a right relationship with God through blood sacrifice. In addition, the fellowship offerings which were presented symbolized a right relationship with God. These fellowship offerings also symbolized a right relationship with fellow mountain worshippers as they shared the communal meal of that offering. The book of Joshua tells us that the whole assembly of Israel was present at Mount Ebal. This included men, women, children and the aliens who lived among them. As these Israelites gathered, they recognized that Joshua was obeying God's commands exactly as these instructions had been given to Moses. Even more than that, Joshua was instructing the Israelites to worship God, learn His instructions and follow the right path.

After Joshua had built the altar and offered the sacrifices, *"Joshua copied on stones the law of Moses"* (Joshua 8:32). This mountain man of God did not stop there. He also read all the words of the law as it had been written. Joshua wanted the people to know the significance of these stones which provided a way to keep on the path of God. The Israelites had entered a land where it would be easy to get off the trail. These mountain people would need to keep their eyes focused on the trail-marker of God's law to keep in step with God's plans so that they could conquer the land which they had just entered.

As I think back to the cairn on the Bridger Mountains, I am thankful for the marker that showed my granddaughter and me the way to Sacagawea Peak. I am also grateful that I could worship God on that mountain without having to build an altar. Most of all, I am thankful that the sacrifice that Jesus offered on Mount Calvary was complete and sufficient to give me a right relationship with God and to point the way to a right relationship with others. Joshua showed the Israelites how to stay on the right path. Joshua was an Old Testament representative of Jesus. This Jesus not only points the way; Jesus IS the Way, the Sacrifice, the Rock, the fulfillment of the Law, and the Builder of relationship with God and with our fellow hikers on earth.

Cairns, altars, monuments, stones, and Joshua are meaningful markers; but none is as meaningful as Jesus, the Rock of my Salvation.

Reflections: Read Deuteronomy 27, Deuteronomy 28:1-14 and Joshua 8:30-35.

1. What other stories in the first five books of the Bible tell about the significance of stones used as marker? (see Genesis 31:44-53 and Exodus 24:4)

2. Compare Deuteronomy 27:12-13 with Joshua 8:33. What impresses you about the way the people were standing?

3. How did the people respond to the curses which were read in Deuteronomy 27?

4. How do you respond to the blessings in Deuteronomy 28?

5. How are the words of God's law a guide for your relationships with God and a guide for your relationships with other people?

Deborah, a prophetess, . . . sent for Barak. . . and said to him, "The LORD, the God of Israel commands you. . . lead the way to Mount Tabor."

—Judges 4:4-6

Chapter Seven

Mountain Woman Deborah

Deborah, a prophetess, . . . sent for Barak. . . and said to him, "The LORD the God of Israel commands you. . . lead the way to Mount Tabor."

—Judges 4:4-6

A Montana outfitter website advertises unforgettable explorations led by experienced mountain men and women. Prospective adventures include wilderness lodging, hunting, fishing and mountain hiking. Travelers who explore Montana with outfitters trust that their guides have expertise based on previous experience. The safety and success of wilderness explorations often depend on a plan and on how well the travelers follow the instructions of the outfitter.

The story of Deborah and Barak in Judges 4 and 5 has many of the components of a good Montana outfitter story: a mountain, a river, a tent, tent stakes, campfire song, horses, pursuits, a skin of milk and a plan. When I first decided to write about Deborah as a mountain woman, I thought that she was the perfect "outfitter." She was a leader, a judge, a willing traveler, and was able to execute an adventure. I asked a friend who has worked for an outfitter about the role of the main outfitter. She described the main outfitter as an overseer who supplies everything, who watches over everything and everybody and who has the final say.

As I read Judges 4 again, I saw these action phrases, *"the Lord sold"* (4:2), *"the LORD commands"* (4:6), *"the LORD will hand"* (4:9), *"has not the*

LORD gone ahead?" (4:14), "the LORD routed" (4:15), and "God subdued" (4:23). These descriptions made it very clear to me that God was the overseer of this outfitter adventure. God supplied everything. God watched over everything and everybody. God had the final say. Mountain woman Deborah was a willing member of God's outfitter crew, but God directed the adventure.

The setting for this story is the hill country of Ephraim where Deborah is both a judge and a prophetess during the time when the Israelites "did evil in the eyes of the LORD" (Judges 4:1). God had allowed Jabin, the king of Canaan and his army commander, Sisera, to oppress the Israelites so cruelly that they finally cried out to God for help. God directed Deborah to execute a plan to defeat these oppressors. Geographical components to this story include: Mount Tabor to the east, the Kishon River in the valley and Harosheth Haggoyim to the west (Judges 3 and 4). Deborah directs Barak to ascend Mount Tabor. Barak convinces Deborah and ten thousand men to join him. Sisera is told that Barak has gone to Mount Tabor. Sisera gathers his men and nine hundred iron chariots. They leave their city of Harosheth Haggoyim to pursue the Israelite army. God, the Israelite's Outfitter, intervenes as these enemies cross the Kishon River. Judges 5:21 tells us, "The river Kishon swept them away, the age old river, the river Kishon."

Sisera, his troops and even his iron chariots were no match for this intervention. Barak and his crew descend Mount Tabor to pursue the troops of Sisera who retreat to Harosheth Haggoyim. Sisera abandons his chariot in or near the Kishon River and flees on foot, but is killed by Jael as he sleeps in her tent.

When Israel recognized their need for an Outfitter who was able and willing to watch over them, God responded to their cry for His help. Deborah, Barak, the ten thousand men, Jael and even the river Kishon obeyed the orders of God who supplied everything they needed. God had the final say; but He used His wilderness team to carry out His purposes. As the Israelites gained confidence in the leadership of their God and His outfitter crew, "the hand of the Israelites grew stronger and stronger... "(Judges 4:24). God used mountain woman Deborah as a judge and as a prophetess, but also as a songwriter. Deborah and Barak are so overwhelmed with the success which resulted from obedience to God that they break forth in the song of Judges 5.

> *"I will sing to the Lord. I will sing; I will make music to the Lord, the God of Israel. . . .Praise the Lord!"*

Mountain Woman Deborah recognized her God as a God of mountains and rivers. Deborah's God guided men and women and even nature to accomplish His will.

He still does.

Reflections: Read Judges 4 and 5

1. What circumstances in your life have led you to cry to the Lord for help? (see Judges 4:3)

2. How do you see faith and obedience as key ingredients in this story?

3. What impresses you about Deborah and Barak's song in Judges 5?

4. Compose a song of praise to God for what He has done in your life.

Now a detachment of the Philistines had gone out to the pass at Micmash. . . on each side of the pass that Jonathan intended to cross to reach the Philistine outpost was a cliff. . .Jonathan climbed up using his hands and feet.

—from I Samuel 13 and 14

Chapter Eight

Mountain Man Jonathan

Now a detachment of the Philistines had gone out to the pass at Micmash. . . on each side of the pass that Jonathan intended to cross to reach the Philistine outpost was a cliff. . .Jonathan climbed up using his hands and feet.

—from I Samuel 13 and 14

The name Jonathan conjures up images of the one who was the son of Saul, the friend of David, and the father of Mephibosheth. However, in this story, we get to picture Jonathan as a rock climber who knew his way around mountain passes.

The terms "mountain pass" and "free climbing" are accompanied by visual images in my mind. Having traveled through the Rocky Mountains, I know that a mountain pass is a route through a mountain range or over a ridge. A pass can also be described as a broad place in a canyon where passage is easy. I have traveled many mountain passes; but I have not become a rock climber. However, having friends who are rock climbers helps me visualize the agility and expertise necessary for this sport. In fact, one of these rock climbing friends recently posted pictures on the internet of his free-climbing solo ascent up the rocky slopes of Montana's Beehive Peak.

These photos of Beehive Peak came to my mind when I researched pictures of Micmash Pass. Photos of this area in Palestine resemble some of the images of the rocky canyons we are able to see in Southwest Montana. Consequently, when I read I Samuel 13 and 14, I thought not only about the plot and the characters of the story, but I also imagined the setting. Micmash Pass had military significance in I Samuel. It was an area about eight miles north of Jerusalem and was a battleground site for King Saul's conflicts with the Philistines as the Israelites tried to conquer the land which God had promised would be theirs. In fact, in the opening verses of I Samuel 13, Saul and two thousand of his men were stationed at Micmash. By the end of I Samuel 13, Saul and his troops had left the area. A detachment of the Philistine army was occupying Micmash.

The plot within this setting was a battle not only for this piece of land; but even more, the conflict involved God's victory over his enemies. The Philistines were idol-worshipping enemies of the Israelites. God had made a covenant with the Israelites that He would be with them as they conquered the land that He promised to give them. The Philistines, as an evil nation, were a major obstacle to the Israelites who were commanded to not only conquer land, but also to conquer evil.

Jonathan and his armor-bearer are important characters in this account in I Samuel. However, as we read the account closely, we become aware that the main character is God. At first glance, we might think that Jonathan's decision to fight the Philistines with only his armor-bearer was an impulsive one. However, we read in I Samuel 14:10 that Jonathan depended on a sign from the Lord before he began his rock climb which ended in victory.

We are not told whether Jonathan climbed the rocky mass wearing his armor. We are only told, *"Jonathan climbed up, using his hands and his feet, with his armor-bearer right behind him"* (verse 13). These two young men surprised the Philistine army by climbing a cliff instead of taking an easier route along the pass. The vigorous rock climb was followed by a battle in which twenty Philistines were killed by these two men of God. The Philistines no doubt assumed that a much larger contingency of the Israelite army was following Jonathan and his armor-bearer. However, again, the Main Character of the story fought the battle without additional troops. I Samuel 14:15 and 16 tell us that the Philistine army melted away in all directions because of a panic sent by God.

The setting, the plot, the conflict and the characters in this story from I Samuel are fascinating. Mountain Man rock-climber Jonathan was youthful, agile, sure-footed and brave. However, the key phrase in this interesting account is Jonathan's testimony,

> *Nothing can hinder the LORD from saving whether by many or by few.*
>
> —I Samuel 14:6

This is a comfort for my daily walk with God. May Jonathan's words be your testimony, as well.

Reflections: Read I Samuel 13:23-14:15

1. What impresses you about this account of Jonathan's battle plan?

2. What or who are the Philistines in your life?

3. How will Ephesians 6:10-18 help you with your battle plan for conquering evil?

Saul was going along one side of the mountain, and David and his men were on the other side of the mountainside, hurrying to get away from Saul.

—I Samuel 23:26

Chapter Nine

Mountain Man Saul

Saul was going along one side of the mountain, and David and his men were on the other side of the mountainside, hurrying to get away from Saul.

—I Samuel 23:26

When Meriwether Lewis and William Clark crossed mountains in an attempt to find a route from the Mississippi River to the Pacific Ocean, they encountered native mountain people. The Shoshone Indians were an integral part of Lewis and Clark's success in crossing the Rocky Mountains. Interestingly, the Shoshone Indians occupied areas on both the east side of the Rockies and the west side of the Rockies. The western band of the Shoshones lived in grass huts and hunted small game for food. The eastern band of the Shoshones lived in tepees and hunted buffalo. Decisions about survival were different on the east side of the mountain than they were on the west side of the mountain.

The expeditions of Lewis and Clark are an important part of the history of Montana. Unfamiliar names like Atsinas, Hidatsas, Nez Perces and Wishrams are part of the Lewis and Clark story. The expeditions of Saul and David are an important part of the history of the Israelites. The setting for our story from I Samuel 23 is filled with many names that are probably unfamiliar to us as well. Horesh, Hakilah, Jeshimon, Keilah, Sela Hammahlekoth, and Ziph are all locations mentioned in this passage.

Although these strongholds, hills and cities are not well-known, they provide the locale for Saul's pursuit of David.

The time frame for this story of pursuit is when Saul is the current (and first) king of Israel. David has already been anointed by Samuel to be the succeeding (and second) king of Israel. Saul had started out well. At the beginning of his reign as king, I Samuel 11:6 tells us, *"the Spirit of God came upon him in power."* However, Saul's impulsive and impatient personality soon got him into trouble. After a battle with the Philistines, Saul was at Gilgal waiting for Samuel to perform the priestly duty of offering a burnt offering. Impatient because Samuel had not arrived, Saul, himself, offered a burnt offering. In response, Samuel, who was not only a priest, but also a prophet and a judge, tells Saul in I Samuel 13:13-14,*"You have acted foolishly. . . your kingdom will not endure."*

After Saul realized that his kingdom would be given to David instead of to one of his own sons, Saul began his pursuit of David. Saul's nature was not only impatient and impulsive, but was also filled with jealousy. Saul did not realize how a partnership with David could be important for the benefit of all of Israel. David had killed Goliath, Saul's enemy. David had soothed Saul's restless spirit by playing music for him on a harp. David had proved that he was capable of killing Saul's adversaries, the Philistines. Saul could have taken David as a partner and friend. Instead, Saul divided his time between warring against the Philistines and searching for a way to kill David.

The Philistine people were enemies of Israel. As the Israelites attempted to follow God's command to claim all of Canaan as their promised land, the Philistines stood in the way. Both Saul and David had intense battles with the Philistines. Consequently, a joining of their forces would have made for a strong army. Instead, Saul chose to be an enemy of both David and the Philistines. In the middle of these conflicts, we read, *"Saul was going along one side of the mountain, and David and his men were on the other side, hurrying to get away from Saul"* (I Samuel 23:26). Just like the Shoshones who used different tactics for survival on either side of the Rocky Mountains, Saul and David used different tactics for survival on each side of the mountain in the Desert of Maon. Saul had turned away from God and had turned to human beings for guidance. He depended on the Ziphites to be on the lookout for David. In contrast, David looked not only to other human confidants; he looked especially to God for guidance. He pleaded, *"O Lord, God of Israel, tell your servant"* (I Samuel 23:11).

Intriguingly, God used the Philistines to save David from Saul's mountain pursuit of him. Saul was diverted from chasing David by a messenger's plea, *"Come quickly! The Philistines are raiding the land"* (I Samuel 23: 27). Saul turned his attention back to the Philistines and David's life was spared. David continued to depend on God for his survival. Saul continued to be impatient, impulsive and filled with jealousy. Self-reliance and seeking help from men rather than from God did not work out well for mountain man Saul. I Samuel 31 tells us the account of Saul's failed pursuit of the Philistines and of Saul's ultimate death by his own sword on Mount Gilboa. Studying the life of Mountain Man Saul can teach us about how to avoid trouble.

Reflections: Read I Samuel 23 and 31. Read Psalm 54.

1. What contrasts do you see between Saul and David in I Samuel 23?

2. When you have "Philistines" to fight in your life, with whom do you identify: Saul or David? Why?

3. What do you learn about Saul in I Samuel 31?

4. What do you learn about David in Psalm 54?

5. How has God been your help. . . the one who sustains you?

As she (Abigail) came riding her donkey into a mountain ravine, there were David and his men descending toward her and she met them.

—I Samuel 25:20

Chapter Ten

Mountain Woman Abigail

As she (Abigail) came riding her donkey into a mountain ravine, there were David and his men descending toward her and she met them.

—I Samuel 25:20

When I read the story of Abigail in I Samuel 25, I think of mountain hospitality. The description of Abigail loading donkeys with two hundred loaves of bread, two skins of wine, five seahs of roasted grain, a hundred raisin cakes, and two hundred cakes of pressed figs is a picture of hospitality at its finest.

I recently found a website that listed Rocky Mountain Hospitality with an address at 1104 East Main Street, Bozeman, Montana. Curious about their services, I walked to that address only to find an empty building with a sign on the door that stated, "360 degree Pet Medical has moved to 338 Gallatin Park Dr." I decided that hospitality is not always what one expects. Abigail's hospitality was unexpected.

My husband and I have had many opportunities to extend "Rocky Mountain Hospitality." Our hospitality may hold a few surprises, too. Our proximity to Yellowstone National Park and to breathtaking mountain scenery makes our home an easy "bed and breakfast" for family and friends. We very much enjoy entertaining guests in our home. However, sometimes I ponder my motives for extending hospitality. Often, we share our home in order to give back to those who have been generous with us. Sometimes, we simply want to provide respite and refreshment to those who selflessly expend their energies for others. We also realize that God has given us the gift of hospitality and in using that gift, we honor God. However, there are times when we are worn out and our motive for hospitality is not so wholesome. We might feed, entertain, and provide a comfortable space for others just so that they will appreciate us and our efforts. Sadly, this last reason is a very poor motive for hospitality.

In my Bible, I Samuel 25 is titled "David, Nabal and Abigail." If we look at these personalities and examine the circumstances surrounding Abigail's hospitality, we might gain some insights into her motives for extending hospitality. Verse 3 describes Abigail as intelligent and beautiful. When she brought an abundance of food to David and his men, one of the reasons might have been that she was by nature a gracious person.

Verse 7 indicates that while David and his men were hiding from Saul's pursuits, they had been very helpful to Nabal and Abigail's shepherds. Consequently, Abigail could have extended hospitality as a reciprocal act during sheep shearing when strangers and poor people often were invited to feast with those who sheared the sheep.

Verse 26 indicates that because of Abigail's generosity, God had kept David from killing Nabal in revenge for Nabal's refusing to give food to David and his men. One of Abigail's motives for feeding David and his men was to spare her husband Nabal's life.

Verse 28 indicates that Abigail also had a purpose in sparing David's life, *"the LORD will certainly make a lasting dynasty for my master (David) because he fights the Lord's battles."* Abigail seemed to be aware of God's plan for David to be king of Israel. Her act of hospitality kept David from the consequences that would result if he committed mass murder.

A final motive for hospitality appears in verse 31: *"and when the LORD has brought my master success, remember your servant."* Abigail wanted to be remembered for her generosity. We do not know all of Abigail's motives for hospitality. However, I Samuel 25 does tell us the outcome. Nabal dies; David remembers Abigail. Abigail marries David.

Abigail's hospitality is an interesting component of this story. However, one other attribute of Abigail strikes me. This mountain woman was adept at riding a donkey. In fact, verse 20 indicates that Abigail was riding a donkey down one side of a mountain ravine and David was descending toward her. Later, Abigail again rode a donkey when she went with David's messengers to become David's wife.

These descriptions remind me of another donkey rider. Jesus rode into Jerusalem on a donkey on Palm Sunday. Within the next week, Jesus demonstrated the epitome of unexpected hospitality—he gave everything that he had—including his life. No one's hospitality, not even Abigail's, can compare with the generosity of Jesus. No one's motive can compare with the purity of Jesus' motive. He gave because He loved.

May God help me to do the same.

Reflections: Read I Samuel 25

1. What impresses you about Abigail?

2. How does Abigail dispel David's anger?

3. When has someone extended unexpected hospitality to you?

4. What are your gifts and what are your motives for using those gifts?

5. What does Christ's generosity mean to you?

But David continued up the Mount of Olives, weeping as he went; his head was covered and he was barefoot.
—II Samuel 15:30

Chapter Eleven

Mountain Man David

But David continued up the Mount of Olives, weeping as he went; his head was covered and he was barefoot.
—II Samuel 15:30

One of my favorite hikes near Bozeman, Montana is an ascent through a forest canopy and along a rock wall cliff on a trail called "Sypes Canyon Trail." Along that picturesque trail is a resting stop which provides a spectacular overlook of the city of Bozeman and the surrounding Gallatin Valley. One summer afternoon, I sat there with my Bible and my "Reflections Journal." As I looked over the valley below, I reflected that even though physically I was sitting near a mountaintop; emotionally, I was in a valley of lament. Reading several Psalms of Lament helped me gain a renewed perspective of God's faithfulness during all seasons of life.

David was a writer of many of these Psalms of Lament. II Samuel 15 gives us a picture of one of the times that inspired his writing. As King David climbed the Mount of Olives in this story, his head is covered, but likely not with a crown. His feet are as bare as the feet of a mountain goat. If he had taken the time to look through his tears, David's view from the Mount of Olives would have given him an overview of the city of Jerusalem and the surrounding valley. The author of II Samuel does not tell us if David's tears are ones of repentance or ones of grief. This passage does tell us that David is fleeing from his son Absalom who is conspiring to be king. Family relationships are in shambles. David's son, Amnon, raped his half-sister,

Tamar, who was also David's daughter. David's son, Absalom killed his half-brother, Amnon, for raping his sister, Tamar. Absalom then went into seclusion for three years, but after his return to Jerusalem, Absalom gathered followers who proclaimed him king in Hebron.

Just like David had been on the run from King Saul many years earlier, David is now on the run from his own son Absalom. David has much about which to lament. Other circumstances in David's life caused him grief, as well. II Samuel 1:17-27 records David's lament after both Saul and Jonathan (David's best friend) died. Psalm 51 records David's groaning after he was confronted about his adultery with Bathsheba and his murder of Uriah. After the II Samuel 15 incident, we read about Absalom's death and David's grief related to that.

Therefore, David's tears on the Mount of Olives are only a few of his tears. His life was full of lament about broken relationships with human beings and about feeling separated from God. However, the wonderful thing about David is that he never stays "stuck" in grief. A close examination of David's cries of lament reveals that within each expression of groaning is also a steadfast expression of God's faithfulness. David's grief consistently brings him to a restoration of relationship with his God of the Mountains. David freely cries out to God, questions God, complains to God and even expresses anger at God.

However, in the midst of groaning and lament, David recognizes God's attributes, God's promises, God's past protection and God's deliverance. David's lament and tears become acts of worship.

King David who climbed the Mount of Olives was the forerunner of Jesus who also lamented near the Mount of Olives, *"My soul is overwhelmed with sorrow to the point of death"* (Matthew 26:38).

King David's lament could become worship because of Jesus who later came to earth to restore broken relationships. While dying on the mountain called Calvary, Jesus lamented, *"My God, My God, Why have you forsaken me?"* (Matthew 27:46).

Jesus' crucifixion groaning also claimed a steadfast hope. After His lament, Jesus declared to David's God, *"Father, into your hands I commit my spirit"* (Luke 23:46). David lamented; Jesus lamented; we lament. But with lament, we must always declare hope in God who is our Father, our King, our Refuge, our Summit, and our Redeemer.

Reflections: Read II Samuel 15:30, Psalm 3 and Psalm 13.

Rev. Mary Bos, a pastor at Central Reformed Church in Grand Rapids, Michigan, has ministered to many people who have experienced grief and loss. She has identified various components/characteristics within Psalms of Lament:

> Address to God
>
> Complaint
>
> Confession of Trust
>
> Petition for Deliverance
>
> Words of Assurance
>
> Vow to Praise

1. Read Psalm 3.

   With which of the above components of a Psalm of Lament can you identify?

2. Read Psalm 13.

    With which of the above components of a Psalm of Lament can you identify?

3. Compose your own Psalm of Lament:

    Address God:

    State a complaint:

    Express trust in God:

    Ask God for a response to your complaint:

    State what you know to be true about God:

    Promise God your praise:

*You who bring good tidings to Zion, go up on a high
mountain. You who bring good tidings to Jerusalem, lift up
your voice with a shout, lift it up, do not be afraid; say to the
towns of Judah, "Here is your God!"*

—Isaiah 40:9

Chapter Twelve

Mountain Man Isaiah (part 1)

You who bring good tidings to Zion, go up on a high mountain. You who bring good tidings to Jerusalem, lift up your voice with a shout, lift it up, do not be afraid; say to the towns of Judah, "Here is your God!"

—Isaiah 40:9

The fortieth chapter of Isaiah seems to start out with a gentle, tender whisper, *"Comfort, comfort my people, says your God."* By Isaiah 40:3, we hear the *"voice of one calling."* By the sixth verse of Isaiah 40, the tone increases to *"A voice says, 'Cry out'."* The intensity escalates even further in Isaiah 40:9 where we hear *"lift up your voice with a SHOUT."*

The command is not only to shout, but to shout from a mountain top.

"Shouting from the Mountaintop" is a story about four moms who climbed Mt. Ranier in Washington State to protest a coal-fired power plant (August 8, 2010 www.emagazine.com/dailynews /shouting-from-the-mountaintop). The climb was strenuous and the "shout" was actually a banner placed at the summit which stated "COAL KILLS." The Mountain Mamas carried their message with courage and with resolve to make a difference.

Mountain Man Isaiah also delivered a message with courage and with a resolve to make a difference. Isaiah's message was also delivered with a shout. However, Isaiah's message was not from himself, but from God.

His message was not proclaimed in Washington State, but was proclaimed in the city of Jerusalem in the land of Judah. His message was not time-limited, but was a message for then, for now and for future generations. Isaiah's message was not "Coal kills." Isaiah's message was *"Here is your God!"* Notice that the shout is not, "Here WAS your God" nor "Here WILL BE your God." *"Here IS your God"* is a message that is current for all generations.

The people of Isaiah's time needed this message of hope and comfort, since they were under attack from Assyria. Isaiah came to them as a prophet commissioned by God to bring words of both challenge and comfort. Isaiah chapters 1 and 2 tell us that God had spoken to Isaiah in a vision with a message concerning Jerusalem and Judah. The mountain city of Jerusalem is significant for many reasons. In Isaiah's time, Jerusalem was considered to be the dwelling place of God. Centuries later, Luke describes Jerusalem as the city where the crucified Jesus rose from the dead. Jerusalem is also identified in Revelation 21:10 as the name of the city where believers will live for all of eternity.

The shout from a mountaintop, "Here is your God" was and is relevant for each of these periods of time. Isaiah wanted to assure the people of his day that God is a God who is a Glorious, Powerful, Everlasting Comforter even when they as a people are weak, tired, weary, and in danger of being carried away into exile.

In shouting, *"Here is your God,"* Isaiah also spoke a prophecy for the future. Isaiah 9:6-7 foretells, *"Unto us a child is born, to us a son is given. . . He will reign on David's throne and over His Kingdom."* Isaiah 40:11 describes that Child, that Son, that King as a Shepherd who tends His flock and gathers lambs in His arms. For those who are weak and weary, Isaiah foretells that His Powerful, Comforting, Shepherding God would take the form of humanity as Jesus, Savior, Immanuel—God with us---a fulfillment of *"Here is your God."*

However, Isaiah's prophecy went even further into the future. In Isaiah 65, Mountain Man Isaiah shouts to the weak and the weary,

*Behold, I will create new heavens and a new earth . . . for
I will create Jerusalem to be a delight and its people a joy. I
will rejoice over Jerusalem and take delight in my people; the
sound of weeping and of crying will be heard in it no more.*

In that new Jerusalem, those who believe in Jesus as their Savior will be
able to finally shout with people from all centuries and from all nations,
"Here is your God." The comfort in heaven, the new Jerusalem, will be
secure because all who live there will hear a LOUD voice saying,

*Now the dwelling of God is with men and He will live with
them. They will be his people and God himself will be with
them and be their God. He will wipe away every tear from
their eyes. There will be no more death or mourning or crying
or pain.*

—Revelation 21:4.

With courage and with a resolve to make a difference in a world full of
weak and weary people, may we not only know this God of Comfort, may
we also shout from the mountaintop, *"MY God is here! Here is YOUR God!"*

Reflections: Read Isaiah 40.

1. What do Isaiah 40: 6-8 and 21-24 tell us about mankind?

2. What do each of these sections from Isaiah 40 tell us about God?

    Verses 9-11:

Verses 12-20:

Verses 21-24:

Verses 25-29:

3. What comfort do you gain from Isaiah 40:30-31?

4. In your daily life, how can you shout, "Here is your God"?

"This is my Father's world and to my listening ears all nature sings and round me rings the music of the spheres."
(Maltbie B. Babcock, 1901)

Chapter Thirteen

Mountain Man Isaiah (part 2)

Shout for joy, O heavens; rejoice, O earth; burst into song, O mountains.

—Isaiah 49:13

You will go out with joy and be led forth in peace; the mountains and the hills will burst into song before you.

—Isaiah 55:12

My husband and I enjoy visiting Yellowstone National Park during each season of the year. During the winter, the snowy branches on the pine trees seem to dance a minuet. During spring, meadow flowers play an arpeggio. Summer brings a chorus of geysers, hot springs and fumaroles. During a memorable fall trip through Yellowstone, we heard the distinctive bugle calls of elk as well as the penetrating sound of steam escaping from Roaring Mountain. Each time we see and hear God's creative wonders in this mountainous setting, we want to sing, "This is my Father's world and to my listening ears all nature sings and round me rings the music of the spheres" (Maltbie B. Babcock, 1901).

The prophet Isaiah never visited Yellowstone National Park and he never sang Babcock's hymn. However, Isaiah was intimately familiar with the songs of nature. Isaiah was called by God to write to the people of Israel. Isaiah's writings have been preserved for us in a book of the Bible named after him. This book of Isaiah is considered to be a book of prophecy. The wonder of Biblical prophecy is that it is relevant not only for the time in which it was written, but also for any future time.

Consequently, reflections about "Mountain Man Isaiah" will focus on how the book of Isaiah is relevant for us today. Isaiah Chapters 49 and 55 contain mountain imagery. These chapters also contain God's call to us to listen to His Word and to respond in faith. Finally, these chapters contain God's call to nature to lead us in a celebration of joy.

God's call to us to listen is clear: *Listen to me. . . hear this. . . now the Lord says. . . this is what the Lord says. . . listen, listen to me. . . give ear and come to me. . . hear me. . .* declares the Lord.

These phrases throughout Isaiah chapters 49 and 55 are not only a <u>call</u> to listen; they <u>command</u> us to be listeners. The reason we have to listen is also clear. God tells us that His suffering Servant, Jesus Christ, is the only One through whom salvation, restoration and comfort are possible. God wants us to listen to the message that He is a covenant God who keeps His promises and who accomplishes his purposes.

God commands us to listen in faith and respond in obedience because He is a God of mercy who will pardon our sins. Isaiah heard these words from God and in turn proclaimed these promises to the people of his day and to the people of our day.

Isaiah, a song-writing prophet, becomes a mountain man prophet as he hears God's call to celebrate the wonderful work of the suffering Servant. God, through Isaiah, first calls on the mountains to burst into song, as we read in Isaiah 49. Then God, through Isaiah, promises that those mountains <u>will</u> burst into song, as we read in Isaiah 55.

Isaiah continues to call us today to listen and to listen well to God's word about the work of the suffering Servant, Jesus Christ. Isaiah continues to call us to respond with faith and in obedience. Isaiah also continues to call us today to celebrate with joy. The next time you are near a mountain, listen to its songs. The next time you see the heavens, remember that this is your Father's world. All nature sings in celebration of Who God is. The earth rejoices in celebration of what God has done, is doing and will do.

May our God of the mountains help us to listen well and to respond with shouts of joy!

Reflections: Read Isaiah 49:13 and Isaiah 55

1. Why are the mountains called to sing in Isaiah 49:13?

2. What promises do you hear in Isaiah 55?

3. How do you visualize the word pictures in Isaiah 55:12-13?

4. What is your personal response to God's commands to listen and to rejoice?

Elijah climbed to the top of Mount Carmel, bent down to the
ground and put his face between his knees.

—I Kings 18:42

Chapter Fourteen

Mountain Man Elijah

"Now summon the people from all over Israel to meet me on Mount Carmel."

—I Kings 18:19

Elijah climbed to the top of Mount Carmel, bent down to the ground and put his face between his knees.

—I Kings 18:42

Mountain man Elijah was a prophet of God during a dismal time in the history of Israel. Geographically, God's people had been divided into the two tribes in the southern part of Canaan and the ten tribes in the northern part of Canaan known as Samaria. The northern tribes, now known as the tribes of Israel, were under the rule of King Ahab. Politically, these ten tribes made alliances with Ethbaal, king of the Sidonians, when Ahab married Ethbaal's daughter, Jezebel. This marriage was a key factor in the spiritual downfall of Ahab and his kingdom. Israel followed Jezebel and Ahab in the worship of Baal in place of exclusively worshipping the one true God.

In the midst of this situation, the prophet Elijah comes abruptly to King Ahab and announces, *"As the Lord, the God of Israel, lives, whom I serve, there will be neither dew nor rain in the next few years except at my word"* (I Kings 17:1). At God's command, Elijah then hides from Ahab during the following three and a half years of drought and resulting famine. God kept His word. He did not send dew nor rain. Because of this drought, the famine in the land became very severe. At just the right time, God again spoke to Elijah, *"Go and present yourself to Ahab, and I will send rain on the land"* (I Kings 18:1).

Elijah went to Ahab. Elijah then called for an assembly on Mount Carmel. By this time in history, Elijah states, *"I am the only one of the Lord's prophets left, but Baal has four hundred and fifty prophets"* (I Kings 18:22). So the "lone prophet" Elijah issued a challenge to the prophets of Baal. He told them that they could call on their god to produce a fire for the sacrifice of a bull. Elijah would call on his God to produce fire. Everyone agreed that *"the god who answers by fire---he is God"* (I Kings 18:24).

The prophets of Baal were frantic in their attempt to get the attention of their god. But Baal did not answer. Baal did not send fire. Elijah, whose name means "God is Jehovah," called the people to him. Elijah then rebuilt an altar that was in ruins. He symbolically took twelve stones and built an altar in the name of the one true God. He had 12 jars of water poured on the offering and on the wood which had been placed on the altar. When he was ready to sacrifice a bull there on Mount Carmel, Elijah calmly prayed, *"Answer me, O LORD, answer me"* (I Kings 18:37).

God answered Elijah with a mighty fire which fell from heaven. The people who had spent the day watching these mountain events fell down in awe and cried "The LORD—he is God! The LORD—he is God!" However, Elijah was not finished with his exhibition on Mount Carmel.

He commanded the people to seize the prophets of Baal, bring them down to the Kishon Valley and slaughter them there. Elijah then took his servant and climbed back to the top of Mount Carmel. There Elijah bent in humility before his God of fire. He repeatedly told his servant to look toward the sea. After the seventh look from the mountain top, the servant reported that he indeed saw a cloud. The sky became black with clouds, the wind rose and the long drought was ended as heavy rain descended from the heavens. Elijah's God of the mountains proved that He was a God of fire and a God of rain.

As I reflect on this story of rain from the sky, this story of a lone prophet named Elijah and this story of our God who is God alone, I think about a mountain peak in Big Sky country. Lone Peak is an elevation of over 11,000 feet. The Lone Mountain area has been developed as a ski resort which caters to thousands of sports enthusiasts. Although I have not put on skis to join family and friends who enjoy the sport, I have watched many people ride the ski lifts up the mountain and descend on two narrow boards at dizzying speeds.

I have wondered how many of those people know my God of the mountains as Mountain Man Elijah did. I have wondered how many of those skiers recognize that there is only one True God and that He is the God of fire, of rain, of snow and the God of them if they believe in His Son as the only Savior from sin. Whether we ever see Mount Carmel or view Lone Mountain, may we learn from Mountain Man Elijah, a lonely prophet, who knew that his God was God Alone.

Reflections: Read I Kings 18

1. What did you learn about Elijah in this chapter?

2. What significance do you see in:

    a.) the twelve stones that Elijah used to build the altar?

    b). the seven times that Elijah asks his servant to look toward the sea?

3. What "Baals" do you worship?

4. How will studying this story make a difference in your life?

From there Elisha went up to Bethel. As he was walking along the road, some youths came out of the town and jeered at him. "Go on up, you baldhead!" they said. "Go on up, you baldhead!" He turned around, looked at them and called down a curse on them in the name of the LORD. Then two bears came out of the woods and mauled forty-two of the youths. And he went on to Mount Carmel and from there returned to Samaria.

—II Kings 2:23-25

Chapter Fifteen

Mountain Man Elisha

From there Elisha went up to Bethel. As he was walking along the road, some youths came out of the town and jeered at him. "Go on up, you baldhead!" they said. "Go on up, you baldhead!" He turned around, looked at them and called down a curse on them in the name of the LORD. Then two bears came out of the woods and mauled forty-two of the youths. And he went on to Mount Carmel and from there returned to Samaria.

—II Kings 2:23-25

This mauling of forty-two youths by two bears is a striking story. Montana newspapers also carry stories of people being mauled by bears. However, hearing of 42 people attacked by 2 bears is extremely attention-getting! "Bear Safety" rules include instructions to hike in groups of four people or more. The rationale behind this rule is that large groups make a considerable amount of noise, appear more threatening to bears and are less likely to attract an attack. So as we read this story of forty two people attacked by two bears, we see that here the rule of "safety in numbers" did not apply. We need to look more closely at the story behind the story.

The setting of this story is a road near the town of Bethel which is approximately twelve miles north of Jerusalem. The name, Bethel, means "House of God." Elisha and his predecessor, Elijah, had recently been in this town together and had been greeted there by a *"company of prophets"*

(II Kings 2:3). The context of this passage shows us that the men in this "company" were prophets of God. However, Bethel was also a town where idolatry and calf worship were taking place.

Characters in this story include forty-two youths from the town of Bethel who taunted Elisha by saying, *"Go on up, you baldhead."* Commentators suggest that these young folks could have been pupils of the leaders of the religion of calf worship. They likely had been aware of Elijah's life as a prophet of the one True God. They no doubt knew that Elisha had now been called by God to carry on the work of Elijah.

Two other characters in this account literally came out of the woods in a frightening attack. These creatures were likely Palestinian brown bears who responded quickly to the call by God to punish those who mocked Elisha, mocked his message and mocked his God.

Elisha is another main character in this narrative. We first met Elisha in I Kings 19:19 when Elijah threw his cloak around this farmer who left his oxen and his family to become a mountain climbing prophet. We next encounter Elisha in II Kings 2 when he accompanied his friend on what becomes Elijah's final trek on earth. As these two prophets of God walk toward the Jordan River, we read three times, *"the LORD has sent. . . . the LORD has sent. . . . the LORD has sent."* This undoubtedly impressed Elisha with the knowledge that the God of Elijah was One who "sent" with control and authority. During this journey, Elisha also saw the power of God in chariots and horses of fire. Elisha saw the power and authority of God in a mighty whirlwind that whisked Elijah to heaven.

Elisha might have felt alone as he picked up the prophet's cloak after Elijah's whirlwind departure. Nonetheless, as he retraces his steps to the Jordan River, Elisha expectantly asks, "where now is the LORD, the God of Elijah?" God showed his power again as this LORD of Elijah, LORD of Elisha and LORD of nature divided the waters of the Jordan River, so that Elisha could continue his walk as a prophet of this One True God.

Consequently, we have to conclude that the main character in this story is not a youth nor a bear nor even Elisha. The Main Character in this story is God. When Elisha called down a curse on the taunting lads, he did it *"in the name of the LORD."* Elisha's God sent bears in answer to Elisha's prayer. After being freed from the taunts, *"Go on up, you baldhead,"* Elisha did go on up! Elisha climbed Mount Carmel where God, years earlier, had proved Himself to be the only true God. Mountain Man Elisha no doubt received strength, energy and insight from his God of the mountains at this Holy Place. We do not read whether Elisha rebuilt an altar at Mount Carmel to replace Elijah's altar which God had burned up with holy fire. We do read that after Elisha spent time on Mount Carmel, he returned to Samaria. Elisha spent the rest of his life proclaiming that His God is the One True God who uses miracles in nature and who uses the words of prophets to accomplish His will and to demonstrate His Almighty Power.

Reflections: Read II Kings 2

1. Note the reference to Elijah's cloak in the following verses:

   I Kings 18:46, I Kings 19:19; II Kings 2:8, 13, 14.

   What do you think is the significance of this cloak?

2. How did Elisha claim God's power in II Kings 2:21 and 24?

3. What did King Jehoshaphat recognize about Elisha as evidenced in II Kings 3:12?

4. Do you have a "Mount Carmel" where you meet God?

5. What could you do to have people say about you, "The word of the Lord is with him/her"?

Solomon began to build the temple of the LORD in Jerusalem on Mount Moriah. . . .He adorned the temple with precious stones.

—II Chronicles 3:1a and 6a

Chapter Sixteen

Mountain Man Solomon (part 1)

Solomon . . . assigned 80,000 to be stonecutters in the hills. . . .then Solomon began to build the temple of the LORD in Jerusalem on Mount Moriah. . . .he adorned the temple with precious stones and the gold he used was gold of Parvaim.

—II Chronicles 2:18, 3:1, and 3:6

My Bible class instructors in both grade school and high school spent a significant amount of time on the details of the construction of Solomon's Temple. We studied the symbolism of the structure of the walls and placement of the furniture within the temple. However, when I read this story while I live in Montana, I have new insights into both the external structure and internal beauty of the temple.

The "alien" or "foreigner" stonecutters instrumental in the construction of the foundation of the temple on Mount Moriah remind me of Croatian immigrant stonecutters who settled and worked in their trade of stone-cutting in Lewistown, Montana in the early 1800's. The description of extensive gold overlays in the temple is more real to me after I have seen remnants of placer mining along Alder Gulch, Montana which was once rich with gold. The adornment of the temple with precious stones reminds me of our trip to Gem Mountain near Philipsburg, Montana where my husband sifted sapphires from that mine's gravel.

However, the external structure and the internal adornment of the temple are only a part of this story about Solomon building a temple of the Lord on Mount Moriah. Just like Montana is rich in history, this temple story is rich in history. Solomon's father, David, was the first king who desired a place where the ark of God could have a more permanent residence. David bought the property for the temple site (II Samuel 24) and made extensive preparations for the building of the temple (I Chronicles 22). However, God, through Nathan the prophet, told David,

> *Are you the one to build me a house to dwell in? I have not dwelt in a house from the day I brought the Israelites up out of Egypt to this day. I have been moving from place to place with a tent as a dwelling. . . . Your offspring. . . .will build a house for my Name.*
> —II Samuel 7:5, 6, 12 and 13

Therefore Solomon is commissioned to build a temple for God's name on a mountain in Jerusalem. His father David encouraged him,

> *Be strong and courageous and do the work. Do not be afraid or discouraged, for the LORD God, my God, is with you. He will not fail you or forsake you until all the work for the service of the temple of the LORD is finished.*
> —I Chronicles 28:20

We can understand that the immensity of the task is not just about the foundation stones, the marble columns, the gold inlays and the precious stones. The immensity of the task of building the temple is actually about structuring a dwelling place for the Almighty God, the creator of the heavens, of the earth and of the entire universe. Psalm 33:13 tells us,

> *"From heaven the LORD looks down and sees all mankind; from his dwelling place he watches all who live on earth."*

Both David and Solomon must have been overwhelmed with the task of building a dwelling place for God's name on a mountain on earth.

Solomon's prayer at the dedication of the temple reveals some of his thoughts about the temple being God's dwelling place. In II Chronicles 6:18, Solomon asks,

"But will God really dwell on earth with men?"

In that same prayer, he pleads with God, *"hear, from heaven, your dwelling place"* and concludes that not only the Israelites, but even the foreigners will know that *"this house that I have built bears your name."*

Theologians point out that God does indeed have His throne in heaven, but He also had chosen a temple on earth for the dwelling place of His name. This temple, this dwelling place, was a mountain site where sacrifices and prayers could be offered in a Holy Place to a Holy God. The temple was where humanity and deity could meet.

Solomon was able to see the completion of the temple. He witnessed the priests carrying the ark of the Lord's Covenant and placing that symbol of God's presence in the Most Holy Place within the temple. Solomon saw the glory of the LORD fill the temple of God (II Chronicles 5:14).

However, the beauty of Solomon's temple cannot compare with God's eternal dwelling place where Solomon, his father David and believers of all ages will see streets of gold and foundations of city walls decorated with precious stones and will hear a loud voice from God's heavenly throne saying,

> *Now the dwelling of God IS with men and He will live with them. They will be His people; and God Himself will be with them and be their God.*
>
> —Revelation 21:3

Hallelujah!

Reflections: Read II Chronicles 2:17-3:7 and II Chronicles 6:1-39

1. What was Solomon's posture during his Prayer of Dedication? (II Chron. 6:13)

2. How does Solomon describe God? (II Chron. 6:14-31)

3. What significance did the temple have for the people? (II Chron. 6: 32-39)

4. Read Ephesians 2:19-22.

   How have you become "a dwelling in which God lives by his Spirit"?

5. Read Revelation 21:22. Why is there no need for a temple in heaven?

God gave Solomon wisdom and very great insight.

—I Kings 4:29

Chapter Seventeen

Mountain Man Solomon (part 2)

God gave Solomon wisdom and very great insight.
> —I Kings 4:29

Then Solomon began to build a temple to the LORD in Jerusalem on Mt. Moriah.
> —II Chronicles 3:1

On a hill east of Jerusalem, Solomon built a high place for Chemosh the detestable god of Moab, and for Molech the detestable god of the Ammonites.
> —I Kings 11:7

Solomon is widely known for the gift of wisdom which he received from God. Solomon is also well known for using his wisdom in the building of a temple for God on a mountain in Jerusalem.

Montana is also known for wisdom. In fact, the town of Wisdom, Montana is located in Beaverhead County which is in the southwest corner of the state. Wisdom was named for the Wisdom River which flowed through the town. Lewis and Clark explored this area in 1805 and named the river as a tribute to one of the virtues of President Thomas Jefferson. Even after Wisdom River became Big Hole River, the town of Wisdom kept its name.

As we read the story of Solomon's life, we see that some of his activities reveal a "big hole" in his wisdom. Solomon started out well. I Kings 2 includes David's charge to his son Solomon to observe all that God requires, to walk in God's ways and to keep God's commands. I Kings 3 tells the account of God giving Solomon a wise and discerning heart in response to Solomon's request for wisdom.

I Kings 6-8 record Solomon's obedience to God in building and dedicating the temple on Mt. Moriah where Solomon's ancestor Abraham had been completely obedient to God in his willingness to sacrifice his one and only son, Isaac.

Solomon's wisdom is evident in both I Kings and II Chronicles. Solomon also is credited with writing much "wisdom literature" including the book of Ecclesiastes and most of the sayings in the book of Proverbs. Psalm 72 is also either written by Solomon or written in reference to him. Even a brief overview of these writings reveals that Solomon knew the importance of whole-hearted devotion to God.

> *O LORD, God of Israel, there is no God like you in heaven above or on earth below"*
> —I Kings 8:23 and II Chronicles 6:14

> *Praise be to the LORD God, the God of Israel, who alone does marvelous deeds.*
> —Psalm 72:18

> *To the man who pleases him, God gives wisdom, knowledge, and happiness.*
> —Eccl. 2:26

> *The fear of the LORD is the beginning of knowledge, but fools despise wisdom and discipline.*
> —Proverbs 1:7

> *The LORD detests the sacrifice of the wicked, but the prayer of the upright pleases him.*
> —Proverbs 15:8

Solomon appears wholly devoted to the LORD God, the God of Israel, whose presence filled the temple on Mt. Moriah. However, there is a big HOWEVER in I Kings 11:1, *"King Solomon, however, loved many foreign women. . . ."* The "big hole" in Solomon's life is identified in I Kings 11:6-8.

> *So Solomon did evil in the eyes of the LORD; he did not follow the LORD completely, as David his father had done. On a hill east of Jerusalem, Solomon built a high place for Chemosh the detestable god of Moab, and for Molech the detestable god of the Ammonites. He did the same for all his foreign wives, who burned incense and offered sacrifices to their gods.*

We enjoy reading the stories about the wisdom of Solomon, the building of the temple and his many wise sayings. That joy turns to grief when we read,

> *The LORD became angry with Solomon because his heart had turned away from the LORD, the God of Israel who had appeared to him twice.*
>
> —I Kings 11:9

Solomon fell into a big hole by building high places for the worship of detestable gods. We wonder how this wise man forgot his own proverb,

> *The fear of the Lord is the beginning of wisdom and the knowledge of the HOLY ONE is understanding.*
>
> —Proverbs 9:10

May our God give us wisdom so that we observe all that God requires, walk in God's ways and keep steadfast so that our hearts do not turn away from Him.

Reflections: Read I Kings 4:29-34 and I Kings 11:1-13

1. What impresses you the most about Solomon's wisdom as described in I Kings 4:29-34?

2. Compare Exodus 34:10-15 with I Kings 11:2. How did Solomon disobey God?

3. In what ways do you compromise whole-hearted devotion to God?

4. Read Proverbs 1:1-7. Consider how reading a chapter in Proverbs each day could aid in attaining wisdom and acquiring a disciplined life.

And Hezekiah prayed to the LORD: ". . . You alone are God over all the kingdoms of the earth."

—II Kings 19:15

Chapter Eighteen

Mountain Man Hezekiah

This will be a sign for you, O Hezekiah: ". . . .Once more a remnant of the house of Judah will take root below and bear fruit above. For out of Jerusalem will come a remnant, and out of Mount Zion a band of survivors. The zeal of the LORD Almighty will accomplish this."
—Isaiah 37:30-32 and II Kings 19:29-31

If King Hezekiah lived today in Paradise Valley, Montana where the Yellowstone River flows between the Gallatin National Forest and the Absaroka Mountain Range, he would see a sign on Highway 540 which says, PRAY.

Isaiah told Hezekiah that he would see a sign. That sign was not a reminder to pray, nor was it a sign like on Highway 540 indicating a location in Montana which is named, "Pray." The sign about which Isaiah speaks is a sign that is in response to Hezekiah's prayer. In fact, Isaiah begins his message about the sign with the words, *"This is what the LORD, the God of Israel says, 'I have heard your prayer'"* (II Kings 19:20).

Hezekiah felt an urgency to pray to the LORD Almighty because Sennacherib, king of Assyria, had threatened to attack and overtake Jerusalem in the same way that the Assyrians had already conquered much of the land inhabited by the ten northern tribes of Israel. I Kings 18-20 is an account of the political situation during this time. These chapters also show King Hezekiah's character and his response to Sennacherib's threats. II Chronicles 29-32 is another record of this time period. These chapters give a more detailed account of how Hezekiah's response included purifying the temple in Jerusalem and celebrating the Passover on Mount Zion. Finally, Isaiah 36-39 tells the same story from the perspective of Isaiah, the prophet of God during these troublesome times in the history of Israel.

Each of these accounts shows that Hezekiah is a king who *"did what was right in the eyes of the LORD"* (II Kings 18:3). Hezekiah was a mountain man in the sense that he held in high esteem the location and symbolism of Mount Zion. This name was used for the temple mountain in southeast Jerusalem, for the whole city of Jerusalem and for the coming Kingdom of Christ as prophesied by Isaiah. In addition to being a "mountain man," Hezekiah was a man who knew how important it is to pray. Hezekiah prayed alone when he heard the news of Sennacherib's plan. In fact, he went to the temple, a place of prayer, to pour out his heart to God. Hezekiah also knew the importance of partnership in prayer. He pleaded with Isaiah, *"Pray for the remnant."*

In initiating a Passover Celebration, Hezekiah called for corporate prayer and worship. Mountain man Hezekiah knew what it meant to pray.

The National Day of Prayer organization uses the acronym P. R. A. Y. to highlight the need to Praise, Repent, Ask, Yield. Hezekiah exemplifies each of these components of prayer in his life.

Praise:

> When Hezekiah and his officials saw the heaps (of contributions for worship), they praised the LORD.
> —*II Chronicles 31:8*

> O LORD Almighty, God of Israel. . . you alone are God.
> —*Isaiah 37:16*

Repent:

> *Then Hezekiah repented of the pride of his heart.*
> > —*II Chronicles 32:26*

> *When Hezekiah heard this, he tore his clothes and put on sackcloth.*
> > —*Isaiah 37:1*

Ask:

> *May the LORD, who is good, pardon everyone who sets his heart on seeking God.*
> > —*II Chronicles 30:18*

> *Now, O LORD our God, deliver us from his (Sennacherib's) hand, so that all kingdoms on earth will know that you alone are God.*
> > —*Isaiah 37:20*

Yield:

> *Submit to the LORD. . . Come. . . Serve the LORD.*
> > —*II Chron. 30:8*

> *King Hezekiah and Isaiah. . .cried out in prayer.*
> > —*II Chron. 32:20*

Because Hezekiah prayed, Isaiah promised him a sign, *"Once more a remnant of the house of Judah will take root below and bear fruit above."* Neither Hezekiah nor Isaiah saw the complete fulfillment of this or further prophecies, *"The LORD himself will give you a sign: the virgin will conceive and will give birth to a son, and will call him Immanuel"* (Isaiah 7:14) and *"He grew up before him like a tender shoot, and like a root out of dry ground"* (Isaiah 53:2). However, we now know that the zeal of the LORD has indeed accomplished answers to Hezekiah's prayers and fulfillment of

Isaiah's prophecies when God *"installed my King on Zion, my holy hill"* *(Psalm 2:6).*

All praise be to God for answering Hezekiah's prayer by sending King Jesus who still instructs us to P.R.A.Y.

Reflections: Read II Kings 18:17-37 and II Kings 19

1. Think about the "remnant" mentioned in II Kings 19:30-31.

   What did this term mean for Hezekiah's day?

   What did this term mean for New Testament people?

   What does this term mean for today?

2. How was Hezekiah's prayer answered?

3. How is Jesus a fulfillment of Isaiah's prophecy "the zeal of the LORD Almighty will accomplish this"? (see also Isaiah 9:6-7)

4. Pray a prayer for your nation using P.R.A.Y as a guide.

"But if you return to me and obey my commands, then even
if your exiled people are at the farthest horizon, I will gather
them from there and bring them to the place I have chosen
as a dwelling for my Name."

—Nehemiah 1:9

Chapter Nineteen

Mountain Man Nehemiah

*"Remember the instruction you gave to your servant Moses. . . .
if you obey my commands. . .I will bring them to the place I
have chosen as a dwelling for my NAME."*
                                        —Nehemiah 1:8 and 9

*"Blessed be your glorious NAME, and may it be exalted
above all blessing and praise. . . .You made a NAME for
yourself, which remains to this day. . . You came down from
Mount Sinai; you spoke to them from heaven. You gave them
regulations and laws that are just and right, and decrees and
commands that are good."*
                                        —Nehemiah 9:5,10,13

Soldier's Chapel in Big Sky, Montana is called a "place of remembrance."
It was built as a memorial to soldiers of the 163rd Infantry division who
died during World War II. Nelson T. Story III was a military man who
remembered Bible lessons read during a difficult time of war in New
Guinea. Nelson T. Story III also remembered his precious son, Nelson T.
Story IV, who died in combat early in WW II. In honor of his son and
fellow soldiers, Story designed the Soldier's Chapel as a place of worship
with an unforgettable view of Lone Mountain. Story also had a memorial
plaque placed in front of the chapel. This bronze plaque honors his son
and lists the names of all the Montana soldiers of the 163rd division who
died in WW II.

Nehemiah was also a man who had a place of remembrance. He remembered the conflicts of the Israelites when they were led away into captivity by the Babylonians. Nehemiah remembered the God of the Israelites who had brought them to Jerusalem to build a temple as a dwelling place for His name.

Nehemiah was also a designer and builder. While living in Babylon, Nehemiah heard that the walls of Jerusalem were broken down. God heard Nehemiah's prayers to return to Jerusalem, so that he could oversee the rebuilding of the walls. These walls would protect the rebuilt temple, so that the dwelling place of God's name could again be a holy place of worship.

Nehemiah did not place a plaque outside the temple; however, the book of Nehemiah is filled with lists of names. Nehemiah chapter three lists the names of those who repaired the gates of the walls of Jerusalem. Nehemiah chapter seven includes a detailed list of the names of the exiles who returned to Jerusalem and Judah after they had been in captivity. Nehemiah chapter ten lists the names of all the people who sealed the renewal of the covenant to follow the law of God given through Moses.

Many of these names had significant meanings:

Nehemiah: Jehovah (the covenant God) establishes.

Meshezabel: God is the One who delivers (Neh. 3:4)

Jozabad: Jehovah has granted (Neh. 11:16)

Joiarib: May Jehovah defend the case (Neh. 12:6)

Jonathan: Jehovah has given (Neh. 12:14)

Despite all the lists of names, the most important name in the book of Nehemiah is **God**. In fact, Nehemiah reminded God of His name in his prayer,

> *You made a name for yourself, which remains to this day. . . .*
> *You came down on Mount Sinai.*
>
> —Neh. 9:10b and 13a

Nehemiah was a mountain man because he recalled that when God came down on Mount Sinai, God revealed His name, *"I AM the LORD, your God"* (Ex. 20:2).

Nehemiah could not see Mount Sinai from the mountains of Jerusalem. However, Nehemiah had a historical view of that mountain. Nehemiah remembered that God had established his covenant with the people of Israel on Mt. Sinai. Nehemiah reminded God that He was a God who dwelt in a temple built for His Name. Nehemiah knew that God is a God who calls each of His children by name and cares about those names enough to preserve them throughout history.

Nelson T. Story III and Nehemiah both knew grief. Nelson T. Story III and Nehemiah both knew the importance of remembering and preserving names. Nelson T. Story III and Nehemiah were both mountain men who took great comfort in worshipping God within the view of a mountain whether it was a mountain of remembrance or a mountain of God's promise.

Reflections: Read Nehemiah 9.

1.   Describe how the Israelites confessed their sins (verses 1-4).

2. What names and attributes of God are identified in verses 5-15?

3. What cycles of the people's arrogance and God's forgiveness do you see in vs 16-37?

    What do these cycles tell you about God?

4. Read Revelation 3:5 and 12. What do you learn there about your name?

    What is your response?

"There is a mine for silver and a place where gold is refined. Iron is taken from the earth, and copper is smelted from the ore."

—Job 28:1-2

Chapter Twenty

Mountain Man Job (part 1)

"There is a mine for silver and a place where gold is refined. Iron is taken from the earth, and copper is smelted from the ore. . . .Man's hand assaults the flinty rock and lays bear the roots of the mountains. He tunnels through the rock; his eyes see all the treasures. . . .But where can wisdom be found? Where does understanding dwell?"
                                    —Job 28: 1, 2, 9, 10 and 12

Job is identified as a man from the land of Uz. Although scholars do not agree on the exact location of the land of Uz, we can easily conclude from Job's descriptions in Job 28 that he was very familiar with mining operations.

As I studied Job 28, I recalled the tour in an underground mine that my husband and I took while exploring the "World Museum of Mining" in Butte, Montana. We learned that gold, silver and copper mining all took place in this mountainous area which is often called "the richest hill on earth." During our tour we were fitted with lamps on our heads attached to battery pack belts. With our head lamps lighting the way, we walked down mine shafts to view veins which had once been rich with minerals. At one point in the tour, we were asked to turn off our headlamps so that we could experience black darkness.

Job is a mountain man who described *"blackest darkness"* as it related to mountain mining (Job 28:3). Job also is a mountain man who knew darkness of the soul. The book of Job describes his initial prosperity, his losses, his testing, the advice he received from his friends, his testimony and his unwavering trust in God even when he was in the midst of darkness.

Even though Job's friends thought they gave wise answers to Job's situation, Job knew that they were not wise. Job uses the mining metaphor to refer to the skill that men show in searching the depths of the earth to find treasures. Job goes on to say that men may use their knowledge for many explorations and men may be able to bring hidden things to light, but man must still ask, *"Where can wisdom be found?"*

Job describes his God as the only One who sees deeply enough to know where wisdom dwells. Job does not understand his suffering. Job certainly is not aware of the treasures that will yet be his. However Job does know the rich truth of *"The fear of the Lord—that is wisdom, and to shun evil is understanding"* (Job 28:28).

As Job searches for wisdom and understanding, he knows that his friends do not have the answers. Job recognizes that God Who seems to be silent. . . Who seems to be further away than the deepest mine shaft. . . Who is somewhere hiding in the darkness. . . his God still is the source of wisdom. In fact after Job asks, *"Where does wisdom come from?"* He gives his own answer, *"God understands the way to it and he alone knows where it dwells."* Job even compared man's assessment of miner's gold to God's assessment of wisdom, *"He looked at wisdom and appraised it; He confirmed it and tested it."*

Job knew that God is the source of wisdom. Yet, Job longed for God's wisdom to be visible in his life. Job recalled the time when God's wisdom was the *"lamp (that) shone upon my head."* Job remembered the past when *"by His light I walked through the darkness!"* Job longed for God's wisdom to be his light in this time of darkness. Despite the desperation of darkness, Job is resilient. However, he pleaded that God would soon again say, *"Let there be light"* (Genesis 1:3). As Job waited with longing, he resolutely said, *"I will maintain my righteousness and never let go of it; my conscience will not reproach me as long as I live"* (Job 27:6). Just as a miner *"brings hidden things to light"*, Job held on to his God. In His own time, God accepted Job's prayers, *"made him prosperous again"* and gave him the comfort of family and friends who *"each gave him a piece of silver and a gold ring"* (Job 42:10 and 11).

Butte, Montana might claim that it once was the richest hill on earth; however, anyone who receives God's Wisdom and Light is richer by far.

Reflections: Read Job 28 and 29:1-6

1. What do you learn about wisdom in Job 28:12-19?

2. What do you learn about wisdom in Job 28:20-28?

3. What do you learn about wisdom in Proverbs 8:12 and 22-26?

4. What insight have you gained from times of darkness in your life?

5. From studying this passage in Job, what relationships do you see between wisdom and light?

"Do you know when the mountain goats give birth?"

—Job 39:1a

Chapter Twenty One

Mountain Man Job (part 2)

> *"Do you know when the mountain goats give birth? Do you watch when the doe bears her fawn?"*
>
> —Job 39:1

Job chapter 38 starts out with the words, *"Then the LORD answered Job out of the storm."* The "answer" that follows is filled with rhetorical questions, delightful descriptions, picturesque narrations and the silencing declaration,

> *"Everything under heaven belongs to me."*
>
> —Job 41:11

Job has experienced immense suffering, feelings of abandonment, inconsiderate friends, and silence from God. God finally comes and tells Job things that Job admits are *"too wonderful for me to know."*

Among those things that are *"too wonderful to know"* is where the mountain goats give birth. Maybe we have never wondered where mountain goat babies are born. Maybe we have never thought about the fact that God indeed sees the birth of each goat kid. However, God asks Job the question, *"Do you know when the mountain goats give birth?"* This question helps Job begin to think beyond his own struggles. God desires that Job's focus be on the Creator, His Creation and His Creatures.

The reality that God knows the location of every mountain goat became a fascinating truth while we were on a family trip to Glacier National Park in Northwest Montana. During a time of planning, our eight year old grandson had listed "Goat Lick Overlook" on his "must see list." He had studied the features of mountain goat hoofs which provide extra traction to prevent the goats from skidding on the rocks. Consequently, we travelled on Highway 2 through the Great Bear Wilderness area. When we arrived at the "Goat Lick Overlook" parking lot, our grandson ran down the boardwalk in great anticipation of seeing dozens of mountain goats licking salt from the mineral laden cliffs. With binoculars in hand, we stood on the viewer stand which overlooks the Middle Fork of the Flathead River. To our family's disappointment, there were no mountain goats within our view.

In a paraphrase of God's question to Job, God seemed to be saying to us, *"Do you know where the mountain goats are?"*

Although we had not seen mountain goats at the overlook, we went to our next destination, *"Running Eagle Falls Nature Trail."* This trail had no disappointments at all. We hiked to the falls, enjoyed the marvelous mountain beauty, listened to the birds, and heard God say,

> *"Does the eagle soar at your command and build his nest on high? He dwells on a cliff and stays there at night; a rocky crag is his stronghold."*
>
> —Job 39:27-28

At our grandson's urging, we stopped once more at the Goat Lick Overlook on our return route. Again, we were disappointed—God knew where the mountain goats were, but we did not!

The next day, we ventured on Glacier National Park's *"Going to the Sun Road."* While viewing unforgettable landscape, pristine lakes, snow-covered mountain peaks, road-hugging cliffs and glacier-frosted rocks, we heard God ask,

"Where were you when I laid the foundations of the earth?"
—*Job 38:4*

"Have you comprehended the vast expanses of the earth?"
—*Job 38:18*

"Have you entered the storehouses of the snow?"
—*Job 38:22*

"From whose womb comes the ice?"
—*Job 38:29*

Suddenly, we heard our grandson shout, "There they are!" We all gazed with glee at mountain goats agilely navigating the mountainside! Those mountain goats had not been at the goat licks where we anticipated them to be. However, God knew all along where they were and He, our generous Creator, gave us the delight of seeing these sure-footed, bearded creatures.

We do not know if Job ever saw a mountain goat or any of the numerous creatures God mentions in His wonderful discourse. We do know that after Job focused on the wonders of God instead of focusing on his own misery, Job made the sacrifices which God requested. Job prayed for his friends and he was restored to a life full of *"things too wonderful for him to know."* I am certain that Job never forgot that his Creator alone knew the divine purpose, plan and place of all creation and all creatures. When we face difficult circumstances, may we, too, hear our Creator God, say, *"everything under heaven belongs to me"* (Job 41:11). May we trust in His care and control over all things.

Reflections: Read Job 38, 39, 40:1-5 and 42:1-6

1. Out of what storm (Job 38:1) does God speak to Job?

2.   As you read Job 38, what creative images do you see?

3.   As you read Job 39, what creatures fascinate you?

4.   How does Job respond to God in Job 40:1-5 and in Job 42:1-6?

5.   What is your response to God when God asks you, "Who am I? and "Who are you?"

One day Elisha went to Shunem. And a well-to-do woman was there, who urged him to stay for a meal. So whenever he came by, he stopped there to eat.

—II Kings 4:8

Chapter Twenty Two

Mountain Woman: the Shunammite

So she set out and came to the man of God at Mount Carmel. . . .When she reached the man of God at the mountain, she took hold of his feet.

—II Kings 4:25 and 27

The mountain woman in this story from II Kings is known as a Shunammite. Her name is never furthered identified. However, this Shunammite woman is described in many ways.

As we read II Kings 4:8-14, we find out that this woman is "well-to-do", married, hospitable, generous, thoughtful, and childless. We also learn throughout this chapter that this woman is a woman who has the capability of "holding on."

Shunem was a city southwest of the southern tip of the Sea of Galilee. As one looks at a map of Israel, one can understand why Shunem would be a convenient resting place on a journey from Mount Carmel to the Jezreel Valley, Gilgal and the Jordan River. Elisha was the "man of God" who travelled this route. Elisha was the beneficiary of the thoughtful, generous hospitality of the Shunammite woman.

After reading about Elisha's travels and his guest room at the home of this unnamed Shunammite woman, I thought about circuit preachers in Montana's early history. William Wesley Van Orsdel was a Methodist preacher known as "Brother Van" who ministered for nearly fifty years in Montana during the late 1800's and early 1900's. Stories are told of Brother Van's passionate preaching to large groups and of his compassionate care to individuals and families. I did not find the names of any women who fed and housed "Brother Van," but it is quite likely that as a circuit preacher, he enjoyed western hospitality in the homes of Rocky Mountain pioneers. I can picture circuit preacher "Brother Van" bringing God's Word of comfort and hope to men, women and children just like his predecessor, the circuit prophet Elisha.

The prophet Elisha was a recipient of the Shunammite woman's hospitality. Elisha was also the recipient of the Shunammite woman's trust. As we look at this woman who "held on", we see that Elisha played an important role in her journey of faith.

The first "holding on" event occurs when Elisha promises this childless woman with an aged husband, *"about this time next year, you will hold a child in your arms"* (II Kings 4:16). Just as Elisha promises, the Shunammite woman holds a child in her arms a year later.

That boy grew, but became ill. The Shunammite woman held on to her precious son as he died in her arms. A journey of faith in God became a thirty mile journey to Mt. Carmel. II Kings 4:24 tells us, *"she saddled the donkey and said to her servant, 'Lead on; don't slow down for me unless I tell you.'"* We can picture a woman who holds on "for dear life" as she hurries to her mountain destination.

When she reaches Mt. Carmel, this grieving mother "took hold" of the feet of Elisha, the man of God. In her agony, this nameless woman holds on to the person who represents the Presence of God. She cries out that she will not leave Elisha until he understands the bitter distress that resulted from the death of her son.

Miraculously, God, through Elisha, raises the Shunammite woman's son from death. This mountain woman falls again at Elisha's feet. This time her posture is one of gratitude. Again she "holds on." This time she holds on to her son who once was dead and now is alive.

The Shunammite woman lived many years before the Apostle Paul. However, his words to the Thessalonians were as true for her as they are for us.

> *Respect those who work hard among you, who are over you in the Lord and who admonish you. HOLD them in the highest regard in love because of their work. . .but always try to be kind to each other and to everyone else. Be joyful always; pray continually. . . .do not treat prophecies with contempt. Test everything. HOLD ON TO THE GOOD. . . .May God himself, the God of peace, sanctify you through and through. The one who calls you is faithful and he will do it.*
> —from I Thessalonians 5:12-24

Reflections: Read II Kings 4:8-37

1. How did the Shunammite woman provide for Elisha?

2. How did God, through Elisha, provide for the Shunammite woman?

3. The Shunammite woman held on to her son and to Elisha. She also held on to her land.

   Review II Kings 4:13 and read II Kings 8:1-6.

   What do these passages tell you: about the woman?

   about Elisha?

   about God?

4. What events in your life exemplify God holding on to you as you hold on to Him?

As fire consumes the forest or a flame sets the mountains ablaze, so pursue them with your tempest and terrify them with your storm.

—Psalm 83:14-15

Chapter Twenty Three

Mountain Man Asaph

Make them like tumbleweed, O my God, like chaff before the wind. As fire consumes the forest or a flame sets the mountains ablaze, so pursue them with your tempest and terrify them with your storm. Cover their faces with shame so that men will seek your name, O LORD.

—Psalm 83:13-15

From July 16, 1988 to September 16, 1988, fires in Yellowstone National Park consumed thousands of acres of forest. Lodge pole pine trees were ablaze on the Rocky Mountain slopes. Thirteen major fires were aflame throughout the summer. From the Fan Fire in the northwest corner of Yellowstone to the North Fork fire on the western edge to the Huck Fire near the park's South Entrance to the Clover-Mist Fire on the eastern perimeter to the Hell-Roaring Fire on its Northern edge, this National Park was surrounded by a tempest of raging flames.

In Psalm 83, the songwriter and singer, Asaph, calls on God to pursue His enemies *"as a fire consumes the forest or a flame sets the mountains ablaze."* Asaph sets the stage for this request. He tells God (Who already knows) that the enemy nations surrounding Israel have said, *"Come, let us destroy them as a nation, that the name of Israel be remembered no more."* From Tyre on the north of Israel to Philistia on the west to the Amalekites hovering south of Israel to the tents of Ammon and Moab on the eastern border, this nation was surrounded by alliances of evil.

Asaph calls God to action with his three-pronged plea, *"Do not keep silent, be not quiet, be not still."* Asaph reminds God that in the past, God had powerfully defeated the mighty Midianites and the chariot-commander, Sisera. Asaph also declares to God that He must act again because this is not just a political battle. This first call to action is a spiritual battle, ***"Do not keep silent."*** Asaph reminds God of His own purposes and plans to be the Defeater of evil. This mountain man psalmist boldly challenges God with the phrases, *"Your enemies. . . Your foes. . . alliance against You. . . ."* Asaph calls God, *"my God;"* but he also sees his God as a covenant God who cannot let *"the name of Israel be remembered no more."* God must defeat these evil nations so that Israel AND the surrounding nations will know that God keeps His promises to His children.

In his second plea, ***"be not quiet,"*** Asaph calls God to action for the preservation of His own name. *"Cover their faces with shame so that men will seek your face, O LORD."* *"Let them know that you, whose NAME is the LORD—that you alone are the MOST HIGH over all the earth."* Asaph affirms this in Psalm 79:9 *"Help us, O God, our Savior for the glory of your name."*

Finally, Asaph says to God, ***"Be not still."*** As Asaph calls on God to pursue and terrify His enemies with fire, tempest and storm, we recognize that this Psalm is ultimately a call to justice. The Psalmist Asaph carries out this theme in Psalm 74:22, *"Rise up, O God and defend your cause"* and in Psalm 75:7, *"It is God who judges."* Therefore, demonstrate your justice, God, by destroying the unjust.

We do not understand how God uses nature to demonstrate His will. The Yellowstone fires of 1988 were caused by both human error and by lightning strikes. Theologians argue about whether God causes natural disasters or whether natural disasters occur because of the overall effect that sin has in this world. We do know, however, that God can use whatever He wants to accomplish His purposes. The positive effects of fire in Yellowstone took time to be revealed; but eventually these positive effects included open vistas of mountain beauty, renewal of lodge pole pines and an abundance of light to the forest floor. Brilliant sunlight produced fabulous wildflowers, lush grasses and variegated vegetation.

God accomplished His own purposes in Israel's history, as well. Despite his cry for justice for the land and people of Israel, Asaph recognized God as a God of all the earth when he shouted,

> *Rise up, O God, judge the earth, for ALL the nations are your inheritance.*
>
> —Psalm 82:8

When we feel surrounded on every side by the pressures of evil; we, too, can call on God to act. Because of the saving work of Jesus, our God is NOT silent. He helps us in spiritual battles for the Glory of His own Name and for the sake of His own kingdom. Like Asaph, we can call out to God to protect His people, His Name and His justice.

Reflections: Read Psalm 83

1. What do you think of Asaph as a songwriter?

2. How do you call on God to protect His people throughout the world?

3. How do you call on God to preserve the honor of His Name?

4. In what ways do you call on God to demonstrate justice?

"As surely as I live," declares the King, whose name is the LORD Almighty, "one will come who is like Tabor among the mountains, like Carmel by the sea."

—Jeremiah 46:18

Chapter Twenty Four

Mountain Man Jeremiah

"As surely as I live," declares the King, whose name is the LORD Almighty, "one will come who is like Tabor among the mountains, like Carmel by the sea."

—Jeremiah 46:18

This prophecy with its mountain imagery was placed in Jeremiah's mouth by the King of Kings. God declares that Nebuchadnezzar, the king of Babylon, will come to attack the land of Egypt. Nebuchadnezzar's power and might would be like the mighty mountains of Israel. Jeremiah was called by God to warn the nations like Egypt about their wickedness. The book of Jeremiah is with filled with many word pictures. Events described in this book of prophecy include descriptions of exile, shedding of innocent blood, chains, guilt, punishment and justice . . . all within a mountain setting.

Abduction, the shedding of innocent blood, chains, guilt, punishment and justice are key words in a more recent mountain story. In 1984, two self-described "mountain men," Dan and Don Nichols ambushed Kari Swenson while she was on a training run in the mountains near Big Sky, Montana. They chained her to a tree. Innocent blood was shed when a potential rescuer was shot and killed by one of the kidnappers. Swenson escaped; the Nichols hid in the mountains for five months before they were captured. Justice was served when these men were tried in the legal system and then imprisoned as punishment for their actions.

Justice for Dan and Don Nichols was determined in Montana's legal system. The theme of justice in Jeremiah seems more complex. God, through Jeremiah, states in Jeremiah 46:28, *"I will discipline you but only with justice. I will not let you go entirely unpunished."* However, our just God tempers these words with His promise, *"Do not fear, O Jacob my servant; do not be dismayed, O Israel . . . for I am with you"* (Jeremiah 46:27-28).

The tribes of Israel and Judah had disobeyed God's laws. They had intermarried, had served false gods, had fallen into the sins of the nations around them. God, through Jeremiah, declared that it was time for justice, not only for Israel and Judah, but also for other nations such as Egypt and the Philistines. Jeremiah prophesies that Babylon would be God's instrument for justice. In fact the King of kings who created the mountains of Tabor and Carmel makes the astonishing prediction that king Nebuchadnezzar of Babylon would *"come like Tabor among the mountains, like Carmel by the sea."* Mount Tabor is a striking landmark with considerable height and steep slopes. Mount Carmel towers over the plains and its western edge drops sharply into the Mediterranean Sea. Nebuchadnezzar would tower over Egypt just like these lofty mountains towered over the plains of Israel.

As we read this prophecy, we cannot help but remember that it was at Mount Carmel where God was declared the one true God when the prophet Elijah defeated the prophets of Baal. We remember Mount Tabor as the mountain where Deborah and Barak, through God's interventions, defeated Sisera. As God compares Nebuchadnezzar to these famous mountains, we recognize that God, not Nebuchadnezzar, is in control of all the events of history.

Even though Jeremiah prophesies that Nebuchadnezzar, king of Babylon, would defeat Egypt and would lead Judah into exile, we need to know that God was still the King of kings. God's justice is beyond our understanding. We cannot fathom how God uses an evil instrument to carry out His plan. However, we do know that God, in His justice, carries out His complete plan of restoration and reconciliation. God declares that He is King; He is LORD; He is Almighty. God promises His children, *"I will surely save you out of a distant place, your descendants from the land of their exile"* (Jeremiah 46:27). Nebuchadnezzar, with all his might, does not have the last word.

Just as God promised, some of His children were brought back to Judah after exile. God preserved generations of His chosen ones so that His Heir, a Savior, would be born, not in Egypt nor in Babylon, but among the mountains of Israel. Mountain Man Jeremiah states twice in his book of prophecy,

> *"The days are coming," declares the Lord, "when I will raise up to David, a righteous Branch, a King who will reign wisely and do what is just and right in the land."*
> —Jeremiah 23:5 and Jeremiah 33:15

God's promise for salvation was fulfilled in a way that was beyond even Mountain Man Jeremiah's understanding. Through another King, all God's demands for justice would be met. King Jesus would fulfill all prophecy. That is why God could say to Jeremiah,

> *"Do not fear. . . . I am with you."*
> —Jeremiah 46:28

Reflections: Read Jeremiah 9:23-26; 10:23-25; 21:11-14; 30:11; 46:13-28

1. How do you define justice?

2. Read again: Jeremiah 46:28.

How would you describe God's discipline, justice and punishment?

How does God's justice differ from legal justice?

3. Read Romans 3:21-26

What do you learn from this passage about God's justice?

"*My sheep wandered over all the mountains and on every high hill. They were scattered over the whole earth, and no one searched or looked for them.*"

—Ezekiel 34:6

Chapter Twenty Five

Mountain Man Ezekiel

"My sheep wandered over all the mountains and on every high hill. They were scattered over the whole earth, and no one searched or looked for them. . . . I will pasture them on the mountains of Israel, in the ravines and in all the settlements in the land. I will tend them in a good pasture and the mountain heights of Israel will be their grazing land."

—Ezekiel 34:6,13b and 14

The book of Ezekiel is well known for visions of four living creatures, a parable about a cooking pot and a valley of dry bones. The book of Ezekiel is less well known for this prophecy about shepherds and sheep. Ezekiel himself was a priest whom God called to be a prophet. In Ezekiel 34, God also called Ezekiel to understand the responsibility of shepherds.

First, God tells Ezekiel to prophesy against the shepherds of Israel who have allowed the sheep to be scattered and to wander over all the mountains. God makes it clear that the "sheep" are actually His people. They have been scattered into exile because their shepherd leaders have not been responsible morally, politically or spiritually.

Next, God tells Ezekiel that even though the shepherds have failed the flock, God would not fail His people. As their Shepherd, God Himself would gather them in, tend them, feed them and provide justice.

Finally, God says that in the future, He would send another Shepherd from the line of shepherd-king David who would *tend them and be their shepherd"* (34:23).

Early hearers of Ezekiel's prophecy would have a clear picture of how Israel's exile into other lands could be compared to sheep wandering over all the mountains and on every high hill. Abraham, Moses, David and Job were all caretakers of sheep. I pictured how these ancient shepherds cared for their flocks in wide open spaces when I read the story of a Montana rancher who cares for over 2000 ewes and 3000 lambs in the pasturelands of the Absarokee region of the Beartooth Mountains. These shepherds must be alert and vigilant as they care for their sheep. The leaders of Israel had not stayed alert and vigilant. Consequently, they lost their sheep.

But then, God comes with His wonderful promise,

> *"You my sheep, the sheep of my pasture, are people, and I am your God, declares the Sovereign Lord."*
> —Ezekiel 34:31

God recognizes that human leaders have failed; but He will never fail to be alert and vigilant. Even though God's sheep have scattered, He will eventually bring them back to Israel. God had the Sovereign power to bring thousands of his sheep back to His mountain temple under the leadership of Ezra and Nehemiah. This picture comes to my mind when I hear about Charlie Bair who had over 300,000 sheep on his Montana ranch in the early 1900's. Charlie's years of shepherding came to an end. God's time of shepherding never ends.

God, through Ezekiel, gave a prophecy for that era, but also for all ages. God promised, *"I will place over them one shepherd, my servant David, and he will tend them"* (34:23). We know that God kept His promise to bring scattered people back to the land of Israel when we read in Luke 2: 8, *"and there were shepherds living out in the fields nearby keeping watch over their flocks at night."* We know that God kept His promise to give them a new Shepherd when we read in Luke 2:11, *"Today in the town of David, a Savior has been born to you; he is Christ, the Lord."*

This new Shepherd was One who was always vigilant and alert. *"When he saw the crowds, he had compassion on them, because they were . . . like sheep without a shepherd"* (Matthew 9:36). This Son of David identified himself, *"I am the good shepherd"* (John 10:11).

Surrounded by mountains, I asked retired sheep rancher Sid Dykstra to tell me what made him a good shepherd. Sid replied, "The most important times are lambing and feeding. I was very careful with the little lambs. My wife was also very helpful, but the sheep knew only my voice because I was the one who fed them." This made me think of the Good Shepherd's promise in John 10:27-28a:

> *"My sheep listen to my voice; I know them, and they follow me. I will give them eternal life."*

Sitting by the river Kebar in the land of the Babylonians, Ezekiel heard God's voice telling him to prophesy about mountains, sheep and shepherds. Someday, sitting with Ezekiel by the springs of living water, we will know the complete fulfillment of prophecy. We will see our Shepherd, who became our sacrificial Lamb, sitting on the Throne of Eternity.

> *After this I looked and before me was a great multitude. . . .*
> *standing before the throne and in front of the Lamb. . . . for*
> *the Lamb at the center of the throne will be their Shepherd;*
> *and he will lead them to springs of living water.*
> —Rev. 7:9 and 17a

At that throne, with Mountain Man Ezekiel and with shepherds of all ages, we will cry with a loud voice,

> *Salvation belongs to our God who sits on the throne, and to*
> *the Lamb. . . . .Praise and Glory and wisdom and honor and*
> *power and strength be to our God forever and ever. Amen!*
> —Rev. 7:10 and 12

Reflections: Read Ezekiel 34.

1. What accusations does God make against the shepherds of Israel in verses 1-9?

2. What action words does God use to describe his plan in verses 10 through 16?

3. How does God describe the blessings that his sheep will experience under the care of the new shepherd from the line of David? (verses 17-30)

4. How do you picture yourself "lying down in good grazing land and feeding in rich pastures on the mountains"? (Ezekiel 34:14)

5. How do you picture yourself by eternal springs of living water? (Rev. 7:9-17)

"But the rock that struck the statue became a huge mountain and filled the whole earth."

—Daniel 2:35b

Chapter Twenty Six

Mountain Man Daniel

"But the rock that struck the statue became a huge mountain and filled the whole earth . . . . the God of heaven will set up a kingdom that will never be destroyed, nor will it be left to another people. It will crush all those kingdoms and bring them to an end, but it will itself endure forever. This is the meaning of the rock cut out of a mountain."
—Daniel 2:35b, 44, 45a

Nebuchadnezzar, king of Babylon, had a problem. Nebuchadnezzar, with all his wealth and power, had mental anxiety for which his wealth could not buy relief. Nebuchadnezzar's troubled mind came from a dream about rocks and mountains.

"The rock that struck the statue became a huge mountain and filled the whole earth" is a phrase in the book of Daniel which brings many pictures to my mind. The Rocky Mountains have views such as "Devil's Slide" along US Highway 89. The Rocky Mountains have sloping masses of small rocks known as talus formations. The Rocky Mountains have fascinating outcrops of gneiss and schist as well as massive peaks of igneous rock. However, in all my trips through the Rocky Mountains, I have never seen anything resembling a rock that became a mountain big enough to fill the whole earth.

What Nebuchadnezzar saw in his dream was so out of the ordinary that even his astrologers and wise men could not help him. This is where mountain man Daniel comes in. Daniel grew up in the mountainous land of Judah. He was taken captive to Babylon during early exilic history. God had given Daniel *"knowledge and understanding of all kinds of literature and learning"* (Daniel 1: 17). God had also given Daniel the gift to understand visions and dreams.

Most importantly, Daniel understood that His God's kingdom was an everlasting kingdom. Daniel was living under the rule of an earthly king who did not understand that Daniel's God had ultimate power over all rocks and hills and mountains and kingdoms.

The earthly king of Babylon, Nebuchadnezzar, threatened to kill all his magicians, enchanters, sorcerers and astrologers because they could not tell him what he had dreamed.

Daniel realized that his life was also on the line because he and his friends were considered to be members of the king's wise guys. He knew that the mystery of Nebuchadnezzar's dream could only be revealed by the God who *"reveals deep and hidden things."*

Daniel asked for time.

Daniel asked for prayer support.

Daniel received a vision from God about Nebuchadnezzar's dream. Daniel praised the name of God. Daniel told the king his dream and the interpretation.

Nebuchadnezzar's dream was about an enormous, dazzling statue made of gold, silver, bronze, iron and baked clay. This statue was destroyed by a rock that struck the statue. This rock became a huge mountain and filled the whole earth.

Daniel told King Nebuchadnezzar that this dream was about kingdoms and governments. Daniel acknowledged that Nebuchadnezzar was a powerful king. However, Daniel instructed this Babylonian king that his dominion, power, might and glory came only from the God of heaven.

This God of heaven will eventually *"set up a kingdom that will never be destroyed"* (2:44). The earthly kingdoms represented by the statue would be crushed by the God of heaven who *"sets up kings and deposes them"* (2:21).

Earthly king Nebuchadnezzar heard from Daniel that his kingdom would be destroyed by Daniel's King of kings. In response, this Babylonian ruler acknowledged, *"surely your God is the God of gods and the Lord of kings and a revealer of mysteries, for you were able to reveal this mystery"* (2:47).

The Rocky Mountains might not have a visual comparison to the rocks and mountains in Nebuchadnezzar's dream. Our earthly minds cannot comprehend the grandeur and mystery of God's power. However, with Daniel, we can trust that what God says is true. Our God of heaven will set up a kingdom that will never be destroyed because He is our Rock and our Redeemer (Psalm 19:14). The Kingdom of Mountain Man Daniel's God will fill the whole earth. The Kingdom of Daniel's God will never end.

Reflections: Read Daniel 2

1. Have you ever had a dream that troubled you? If so, what did you do about it?

2. Compare Daniel 2:37 with the descriptions in Daniel 1:17 and 2:23.

    What had God given Daniel that God had not given to Nebuchadnezzar?

3. For what does Daniel praise God in Daniel 2:20-23?

4. How is Nebuchadnezzar's kingdom described in his dream?

   What happens to all of the kingdoms represented by the statue?

5. Read Revelation 11:15-18. How does this passage relate to Daniel Chapter 2?

Like dawn spreading across the mountains, a large and mighty army comes.

—Joel 2:2b

Chapter Twenty Seven

Mountain Man Joel

Like dawn spreading across the mountains, a large and mighty army comes.

—Joel 2:2b

The prophet Joel wrote a book filled with visual imagery. We do not know much about Joel, son of Pethuel. However, we do know that he heard and proclaimed the word of the Lord. We also know that he used word pictures in his role as a mountain prophet.

Joel's word picture, *"like dawn spreading across the mountains"* prompts me to remember a September morning in Montana. My husband and I left Bozeman while it was still dark. We drove east on Interstate 90 for 36 miles before turning north on highway 89. We parked our vehicle along the Shields River. During thirty spectacular minutes we watched the sun rise over the range of the Rockies known as the Crazy Mountains. The sky turned from purple gray to gentle pink to glistening orange. We knew from experience that once the sun started to rise in the east it would continue its circuit until it set in the west.

"Like dawn spreading across the mountains, a large and mighty army comes. . . ." Joel proclaimed that *"the day of the Lord is coming."* This phrase, 'the day of the Lord' is commonly considered to be a description of God's just judgment. Just as dawn comes with a certainty, God's judgment comes with certainty. The phenomenon that God used for judgment during the time of Joel was a plague of locusts.

Joel chapter one provides great detail related to the devastation and destruction that was caused by an army of locust. Joel chapter two adds imagery to the processional of the locusts. Mountain Man Joel goes on to explain that this plague of judgment is actually a call by God for repentance. The book of Joel reminds me of the book of Judges where we see the cycles of: the people rebel; God sends retribution; the people repent; God sends redemption; the people experience a time of rest. The key to this rest is a renewal of their relationship with God.

1. The people have rebelled.

> *Blow the trumpet in Zion; sound the alarm on my holy hill.*
> *—Joel 2:1*

This is a clear wake-up call. Joel announces that God's judgment is necessary because the people have sinned. The people in the land should tremble in fear because of their rebellion.

2. God sends retribution.

> *The Lord thunders at the head of his army. . . the day of the*
> *Lord is great; it is dreadful. Who can endure it?*
> *—Joel 2:11*

God is in control of the locusts and the devastation that they caused. Locusts have caused the fields to be ruined; the ground to be dried up; the grain to be destroyed; the new wine to be dried up and the oil to fail. God sent his judgment (retribution) as a reminder to His people that they have broken their relationship with Him.

3. The people repent.

> *"Even now. . . return to me. . . rend your hearts. . . Return*
> *to me."*
> *—Joel 2:12-13*

4. God sends redemption.

Then the Lord will be jealous for his land and take pity on His people. The Lord will reply to them, "I am sending you grain, new wine and oil, enough to satisfy you fully."
—*Joel 2:18-19*

5. The people experience a renewal of their relationship with God.

"You will have plenty to eat, until you are full, and you will praise the name of the Lord your God, who has worked wonders for you. . . .then you will know that I am in Israel, that I am the Lord your God and that there is no other."
—*Joel 2:26-27*

With Joel, we can enjoy the dawn of each new day. With Joel, we can know that even when we rebel and God sends retribution to call us to repentance, we can have redemption through Jesus Christ. In Christ alone, we have restoration of relationship with our mighty God of the mountains. With Mountain Man Joel, we can be glad and rejoice in the Lord our God.

Reflections: Read Joel 2

1. Rebellion: How have the people of Joel's day rebelled? (Consider Deut. 6:10-12 and Isaiah 2:11-18)

2. Retribution: How has God sent retribution? (see also Joel 1:4-12)

3. <u>Repentance</u>: How does God call the people to repentance? (see also Joel 1:13-14)

4. <u>Redemption</u>: How does God redeem His people in Joel's day?

   -- How does God redeem His people in our day?

   - How does God redeem His people in the future?

5. How do you experience a <u>renewal</u> of your relationship with God when you repent?

He who forms the mountains, creates the wind, and reveals his thoughts to man, He who turns dawn to darkness and treads the high places of the earth—the LORD God Almighty is His name.

—Amos 4:13

Chapter Twenty Eight

Mountain Man Amos

He who forms the mountains, creates the wind, and reveals his thoughts to man, He who turns dawn to darkness and treads the high places of the earth—the LORD God Almighty is His name.

—Amos 4:13

Shepherd Amos became prophet Amos when God called him to pronounce judgments against Israel's neighbors and against Israel itself. Amos 4:13 is a powerful verse which shows that shepherd Amos also became a mountain man who knew God as the One who formed the mountains and tread on those mountains. Amos' God was the Almighty God Who placed His Name on the mountains.

In Montana, we do not see many names written on mountains. However, we do see a lot of individual letters on mountains. Those letters are generally made out of cement or large white-washed rocks and placed on a mountain or foothill near a town. For example, an "A" is clearly visible on a hiking trail near Anaconda. As we have travelled on highways through the Rocky Mountains, we have seen a "D" for Drummond, an "F" for Frenchtown and a "G" for Gardiner. The letter "M" is also frequently seen on the side of a mountain. "M" can stand for Missoula, but also for Montana. Just as these letters represent the name of a town or state, God's name in the book of Amos represents who He is.

"The LORD God Almighty is His Name" is a powerful phrase. The phrase is used seven times in the short book of Amos. The name **"LORD God Almighty"** gives us the sense that God is Sovereign. "Sovereign LORD" is used eighteen times in the book of Amos.

Consequently, if we study Amos 4:13 in the context of God's sovereignty, we see God as the One who formed the mountains and created the wind. We also recognize that God has supreme power and control over all creation and all creatures. In His sovereignty, God turns the dawn to darkness. In His sovereignty, God reveals his thoughts to created beings. God has absolute authority over the high places of the earth. God is Almighty in his dealings with all nations and all peoples.

When I studied God's name as LORD God Almighty, I initially looked at "God Almighty" as "El Shadday" which might be literally translated, "God the Mountain One." This meaning gives me the assurance that God is strong and unmovable. Adding LORD to that name of God assures us that He is also our Covenant God—faithful, always near, unchanging in love, compassion and generosity.

When I studied letters on the side of mountains, I learned that the "M" on Mt. Baldy in Bozeman stands not just for Montana, but also for Montana State University. The "M" on Mount Sentinel stands not just for Missoula, Montana, but also for the University of Montana. My research revealed that University students in both Bozeman and Missoula take great pride in keeping those letters white and visible, since mountainside letters are important symbols.

Further research into "LORD God Almighty" reveals that Amos actually uses the Hebrew words "El" meaning God and "Tsaba" meaning "of the hosts." Therefore, Amos 4:13 talks about God, not as "El Shadday," but as "Tsaba," the Lord of a host of armies. This gives a fuller meaning and evidence of the symbolism behind this Name of God. Tsaba is an all-powerful God who leads out warriors. He is the head of a host of armies in the spiritual realm. In the context of the entire book of Amos, God is a Warrior who pronounces judgment and calls for social justice. Our

LORD God of hosts is One whom we must be prepared to meet as Amos 4:12 clearly states.

The seven references in Amos to "LORD God Almighty" all refer to this Tsaba--"LORD God of hosts" who punishes (3:14), who calls us to hate evil and maintain justice (5:14, 15, 16), who sends into exile (5:27), who stirs up nations (6:14), who touches the earth and it melts (9:5).

This "Tsaba" God called Amos to proclaim His judgment as well as His sovereignty. However, this "Tsaba" God, who created the wind of nature, also is a Holy God whose Spirit came with the sound of wind on Pentecost so that the Holy Spirit even today reveals His thoughts to us.

As LORD of Hosts, God calls us to meet Him, know His name, and through Him seek good, hate evil and maintain justice. Then we can find comfort and not be fearful to know that *"He who forms the mountains. . . . the LORD God Almighty is His name."*

We need to keep that name hallowed and pure. We need to keep that name even more visible than the symbolic white letters on mountainsides in Montana.

Reflections: Read Amos 4:6-13

1. What recurring phrase do you find in these verses?

    What does this tell you about the people?

What does this tell you about God?

2. What does it mean to you that God is the "Lord of a host of armies"?

3. What does it mean to you that the Sovereign, Almighty Warrior God is also "LORD" (Covenant-keeping God)?

4. How does God reveal His thoughts to you?

5. Read Amos 5:14, 15, and 16: How do you seek good, hate evil and maintain justice?

You should not march through the gates of my people in the day of their disaster, nor look down on them in their calamity in the day of their disaster nor seize their wealth in the day of their disaster.

—Obadiah 13

Chapter Twenty Nine

Mountain Man Obadiah

Deliverers will go up on Mount Zion to govern the mountains of Esau. And the kingdom will be the LORD's.

—Obadiah 21

When my husband and I trekked through the ghost town of Granite, Montana, I did not think of the mountains of Esau. However, when I recently read the book of Obadiah, I was reminded of Granite. Following are some of the comparisons that came to mind.

Granite Mountain was given its name because it is formed from solid granite rock. The mountains of Esau were also rocky as evidenced by Obadiah verse 3, *"you who live in the clefts of the rocks."*

The town of Granite has an elevation of 8,000 feet. Our little Buick had a tough climb when we drove on the winding, bumpy road to reach this spot on the map. In comparison, the inhabitants of Edom, in the mountains of Esau, are described as *"you who. . . make your home on the heights"* (verse 3). Historians claim that some of this area could be reached only by climbing through difficult mountain passes.

By the late 1800's, Granite, Montana had become the greatest producer of silver in the United States. The Granite Mountain Mine and the Bi-Metallic Mine employed approximately 7,000 men. The mining business became a source of security and pride. Similarly, mountain man Obadiah states about the Edomites, *"the pride of your heart has deceived you"* (verse 3).

The people of Granite based their security and pride on the fact that, between 1882 and 1893, the mines produced $33 million in silver. In comparison, the people of Edom grew rich because they had control over many of the trade routes of the ancient world. Some of the wealth of Edom was put in vaults in the rocks.

The inhabitants of Edom and the inhabitants of Granite, Montana would both have been wise to heed the truth of Proverbs 16:18,

"Pride goes before destruction, a haughty spirit before a fall."

The mountains of Edom and the mountains of Granite held grand potential. However, both locations became ghost towns whose ruins are still visible today.

Following the "Silver Panic of 1893," miners and their families rapidly exited Granite Mountain leaving it a ghost town. Treading carefully, my husband and I explored mine structures and remnants of buildings, including an old bank vault, in this abandoned town. However, not one person lives in the area which was once booming with silver.

The ancient land of Edom is also in ruins. The city of Petra was the capital of this once proud area. Not one person now lives in this city. Petra, too, has become a "ghost town" with magnificent ruins of a once proud and wealthy metropolis.

I am not sure of the ethnicity of Granite Mountain miners. I know more about the Edomites. These mountain dwellers were descendants of Esau, the twin brother of Jacob. Conflict between Jacob and Esau began even before they were born to Isaac and Rebekah as evidenced in Genesis 25: 22, *"the babies jostled each other within her (Rebekah)."* This long standing controversy becomes the subject of Obadiah's prophecy against Edom where Esau's descendants lived.

Obadiah sees a vision and hears God say,

> *This is what the Sovereign LORD says about Edom. . . . "Will*
> *I not destroy the wise men of Edom, men of understanding in*
> *the mountains of Esau? . . .and everyone in Esau's mountains*
> *will be cut down in the slaughter."*
>
> —Obadiah 1, 8, and 9

Seeing and experiencing "ghost towns" can leave one with a feeling of despair. Seeing Granite, Montana and reading about Edom could also leave one with a feeling of despair. However, Obadiah does not leave us in despair. Mountain Man Obadiah ends his book of prophecy with hope and the promise of deliverance.

> *Deliverers will go up on Mount Zion to govern the mountains*
> *of Esau. And the kingdom will be the LORD's.*
>
> —Obadiah 21

Esau's kingdom failed because Edom became a godless nation full of pride. The warning for us both as individuals and as nations is to defeat pride by recognizing that only God's Kingdom is forever. We recognize that God's Kingdom will never be a ghost town kingdom when we pray:

> *Your Kingdom come, O God; your will be done on earth as*
> *it is in heaven. . . .for yours, God, is the kingdom and the*
> *power and the glory forever and ever. Amen.*

Reflections:

1. Review the "birthright story" in Genesis 25:19-34.

   Why did Esau sell his birthright to Jacob?

2. Review the "blessing story" in Genesis 27:1-41.

   How did Esau feel about Jacob getting the blessing of the firstborn?

3. Read Numbers 20:14-21.

   What does this story tell you about the animosity between the descendants of Esau and the descendants of Jacob?

4. **Read Obadiah** What reasons does God give for destroying Edom?

   Verse 10:

   Verse 11:

   Verse 12:

   Verse 13:

Verse 14:

5. What was God's judgment? (verses 6,7,8,9-11, and18)

6. What was God's final solution? (verse 21)

7. What personal applications can you make after reading Obadiah?

Look! The LORD is coming from His dwelling place; he comes down and treads the high places of the earth. The mountains melt beneath him and the valleys split apart.

—Micah 1:3-4a

Chapter Thirty

Mountain Man Micah

Look! The LORD is coming from His dwelling place; he comes down and treads the high places of the earth. The mountains melt beneath him and the valleys split apart.

—Micah 1:3-4a

You will again have compassion on us; you will tread our sins underfoot. . . .

—Micah 7:19a

God's word came to mountain man Micah while he was living in Moresheth which is twenty five miles southwest of Jerusalem. God came to Micah in a vision of prophecy concerning Samaria and Jerusalem. As we read the words of Micah's prophecy, we wonder what visual images Micah saw as he proclaimed God's Words to the countryside people of his day.

One word in Micah's book of prophecy that gave me a visual image is the word "tread." In fact Micah uses this word twice in relation to God.

Micah chapter 1 tells us that God *"treads the high places of the earth."*

Micah chapter 7 tells us that God *"will tread our sins underfoot."*

Tread. How does God tread? How do I tread? I pondered the word "tread" as I snowshoed in Beehive Basin. I was not walking. I was not hiking. I was not plodding. . . well, maybe I was plodding. I was leaving marks in the snow. Were those marks from my snowshoes "tread marks"? I may or may not have been treading, but I was certainly leaving my mark.

That brought me back to the question, "How does God tread?"

Micah 1 gives the image of God treading in judgment. God comes from *"his dwelling place; he comes down and treads the high places of the earth."* His treading is so powerful that Micah sees an image of nature responding, *"the mountains melt beneath him and the valleys split apart, like wax before the fire, like water rushing down a slope."*

Micah goes on to write that this judgment is because of sins and transgressions involving Jacob, Israel, Samaria, Judah and Jerusalem.

As God treads, He leaves His mark of JUDGMENT.

Back to Beehive Basin . . . as my snow shoes left tread marks, I witnessed the beauty around me. I saw the mountains God made and the valleys God made. I thought about how God's creative beauty responded to His treading in judgment. I wondered, "How do marvelous mountains melt and beautiful valleys split apart?"

As God treads, He leaves His mark of BEAUTY.

I was still thinking about the book of Micah when I returned to the Beehive Basin trailhead. I took off my snowshoes and got into our Mercury Villager with its front wheel drive. I was thinking about the despair of the people to whom Micah prophesied when I was thrust into my own despair. Unfortunately, the narrow road which led back to the main highway was steep and slippery. After several unsuccessful attempts to get our van up the elusive incline, I gave up. I needed rescue. I thought about the rescue promised in Micah 5:2,

"But you, Bethlehem. . . .out of you will come for me one who will be ruler over Israel. . . ."

God did not leave Israel stuck in their sins and transgressions. God sent the hope of a Rescuer. God did not leave me stuck in Beehive Basin either. He sent the hope of a Big Sky rescuer.

As God treads, He leaves His mark of HOPE.

After the Big Sky Tow Truck driver pulled our van out of the snow and ice and towed me to the top of a hill, I paid the bill and was relieved to drive safely to the main highway.

After listening to Micah's prophecy of judgment, mountain man Micah's hearers are relieved to hear these words about the God who treads the mountains,

> *Who is a God like you, who pardons sin and forgives the transgression of the remnant of this inheritance? You do not stay angry forever but delight to show mercy. You will again have compassion on us; you will tread our sins underfoot and hurl our iniquities into the depth of the sea.*
>
> *—Micah 7:18-19*

As God treads, He leaves His mark of RESCUE.

What a Rescuer our God is! He treads the mountains in judgment; but He also treads our sins underfoot! Those tread marks pierced the hands and feet of Jesus as he hung on the mountain of Calvary for my sins and transgressions.

> *The Word of the Lord that came to Micah of Moresheth . . .*
> *the vision he saw concerning Samaria and Jerusalem.*
>
> *—Micah 1:1*

The word of the Lord that came to Mountain Man Micah, God treads with:

Judgment, Beauty, Hope and Rescue

Reflections on the book of Micah:

1. Read Micah 1:1-7. Why did God tread in judgment?

2. Read Micah 4:1-5. Where and why did God tread in beauty?

3. Read Micah 2:12-13 and 7:7. How does God tread with hope?

4. Read Micah 5:2 and 7:18-20. How does God tread with rescue?

5. Read Micah 6:1-2 and 6-8. What is your response?

He stood, and shook the earth; he looked, and made the nations tremble. The ancient mountains crumbled and the age-old hills collapsed. His ways are eternal. . . . the mountains saw you and writhed.

—Habakkuk 3:6 and 10a

Chapter Thirty One

Mountain Man Habakkuk

He stood, and shook the earth; he looked, and made the nations tremble. The ancient mountains crumbled and the age-old hills collapsed. His ways are eternal. . . . the mountains saw you and writhed.

—Habakkuk 3:6 and 10a

When I read these verses during a snowy winter in Montana, I jotted "avalanche" in the margin of my Bible. Historians have recorded stories about avalanches with enough power that massive rocks and robust trees have been swept away by the force of snow hurling down the mountainside. When I read about God shaking the earth so that mountains crumble, I thought about avalanches.

A closer reading of Habakkuk made me think about more avalanche comparisons. In Chapter 1, Mountain Man Habakkuk issues a complaint to God with descriptions of avalanche-like destruction and violence. Habakkuk asks God why He tolerates the injustice of the Jewish leaders. God answers Habakkuk by describing how He will raise up the Babylonians to punish Judah. The Babylonians will sweep across the whole earth like the wind. Sounds like an **avalanche of punishment** to me!

Habakkuk then complains that God is using wicked people to *"swallow up"* less wicked people. Sounds like an **avalanche of justice** to me!

God again responds, *"the earth will be filled with the knowledge of the LORD, as the waters cover the sea"* (2:14). Sounds like an **avalanche of mercy** to me!

This back and forth communication between God and Habakkuk reminds me of another avalanche comparison. Montana has designations known as "avalanche beacon training parks." These parks allow skiers, ice climbers and snowmobilers to prepare for avalanche mishaps. Transmitter beacons are hidden beneath mounds of snow to simulate someone trapped underneath an avalanche. Training for avalanche disaster involves a person using another beacon as a receiver to detect the signals from the buried beacon. One simple goal of the exercise is to teach the potentially trapped avalanche victim to leave his beacon on "transmit" and to teach the potential rescuer to switch his beacon to "receive."

Habakkuk's conversation with God tells me that Habakkuk had already learned his lessons on transmitting and receiving. Habakkuk, like a person buried in the snow, cries out, *"How long, O LORD, must I call for help?"* (1:2). Twice Habakkuk cries out. Twice God hears and answers. Twice Habakkuk listens.

God's beacon is successful in rescuing Habakkuk from despair. Habakkuk sees the light when he hears God say, *"But the LORD is in His holy temple; let all the earth keep silent before him"* (2:20).

In his final response, Habakkuk sings a prayer acknowledging that he is no longer trapped by questions, but that he stands in awe of God's deeds of punishment, justice and mercy.

Habakkuk recognizes that God, in executing punishment, can use even the wicked Babylonians: *"in wrath you strode through the earth and in anger you threshed the nations"* (3:12).

Habakkuk recognizes that God, in administering justice, will ultimately restore Judah: *"you came out to deliver your people, to save your anointed one"* (3:13).

Habakkuk recognizes God's holiness and abhorrence of sin; but pleads, *"in wrath, remember mercy"* (3:2).

Like a skier who has been rescued by a deliverer after being trapped by an avalanche, Habakkuk shouts with rejoicing,

> *"The Sovereign Lord is my Strength; he makes my feet like the feet of a deer, he enables me to go on the heights."*
>
> —Habakkuk 3:19

That is a mountain top experience for an experienced mountain man like Habakkuk who knows that his mountain God is a God of punishment, justice and mercy.

Reflections: Read Habakkuk 3.

1. How does Habakkuk describe God?

2. Notice the two "yet, I will" phrases in verses 16-18.

    What precedes these phrases?

    What follows these phrases?

3. Describe a "yet, I will" time in your own life.

4. God says to Habakkuk (2:4b) "but the righteous will live by his faith."

   What does this mean?

5. Where do you see Christ in Habakkuk 3?

"Go up into the mountains and bring down timber and build the house so that I may take pleasure in it and be honored," says the LORD.

—Haggai 1:8

Chapter Thirty Two

Mountain Man Haggai

"Go up into the mountains and bring down timber and build the house so that I may take pleasure in it and be honored," says the LORD.

—Haggai 1:8

Ghost towns are a reality in Montana even though their namesake "ghost" is somewhat symbolic. Ghost town icons dot the map of Montana. By definition, a "ghost town" is a town that no longer exists. Sometimes, the very location is even lost. However, from time to time, ghost towns are rebuilt. A case in point is Nevada City, Montana.

1863 AD: Nevada City, MT built by miners at the base of the Tobacco Root Mountains

1864 AD: Nevada City and surrounding hill population: 10,000

1869 AD: Nevada City population: 110

1876 AD: Nevada City . . . ghost town

1959 AD: rebuilding of Nevada City, MT by Charles and Sue Bovey

1997 AD: 90 historic buildings along the streets of Nevada City, MT purchased by the state of Montana.

As I studied the book of Haggai and reviewed the events surrounding the building, destruction and rebuilding of the temple in Jerusalem, I thought about Jerusalem as a ghost town that needed rebuilding.

967 BC: Temple built in Jerusalem by Solomon.

586 BC: Solomon's temple destroyed by the Babylonians

537 BC: foundation of temple rebuilt

536 BC: rebuilding of the temple stopped

520 BC: rebuilding of the temple in Jerusalem restarted

516 BC: rebuilding of the temple in Jerusalem completed.

Historians are not in complete agreement about the above dates. However, the Bible tells us with certainty that the temple events did happen.

The Israelites were told to go up into the mountains and bring down timber to rebuild the temple in Jerusalem just like the Boveys in Montana who got lumber and structures from around Montana to reconstruct what had been Nevada City.

In 967 BC, the focal point in the Holy City, Jerusalem, was the temple, God's *"dwelling place"* (II Chron. 6). In contrast, as I toured the rebuilt Nevada City in 2012, I did not see any center for worship. The city includes saloons and a Gallows Barn, but no church. The city has houses and gardens, but has no house for God to be honored.

This same situation was true in Jerusalem in 520 BC. Exiles had returned to Jerusalem after captivity by the Babylonians. They had built homes and planted vineyards. However, they had neglected the rebuilding of the temple. Therefore, the word of the Lord came to Haggai. The Lord Almighty told Haggai to tell the people to rebuild the house of the Lord.

All throughout the history of the Israelite nation, God had called them, *"My people."* Interestingly, in Haggai 1:2, *"This is what the LORD Almighty says, 'these people say "the time has not yet come for the Lord's house to be built."'"* The term *"these people"* reveals that they have distanced themselves so much from the LORD Almighty that they have not longed for a relationship with Him in a sacred House of Worship.

Mountain Man Haggai comes four times with a firm message to the people, *"give careful thought to your ways"* (Haggai 1:5, 7 and 2:15, 18). These careful thoughts had to give way to action. In order for *"these people"* to again become *"My people"* they had to go up to the mountains and bring down timber. This timber had to be used to rebuild a place where God could be honored.

Haggai was obedient in speaking God's words to the residents of Jerusalem. The hearers of the message *"obeyed"* and *"feared the Lord"* (Haggai 1:12). In immediate response, God again declares, *"I am with you"* (1:13). In this amazing response, our covenant keeping God changes *"these people"* to *"My people."* The relationship is re-established even before the rebuilding of the temple in complete.

Today, God comes to us and says,

> *"Don't you know that you yourselves are God's temple and that God's Spirit lives in you?"*
>
> —I Cor. 3:16

May each of us be so in tune with God's Spirit that none of us becomes a ghost town.

Reflections: Read Haggai Chapter 1

1. What excuses did the Israelites give for not building the Lord's house?

2. How had their priorities gotten mixed up?

3. What were the consequences of not putting God first?

4. What were the rewards of obedience? (See also Haggai 2:1-9 and 19b-23)

5. How does your life show that you are filled with the Holy Spirit (Holy Ghost)?

At that time, Mary got ready and hurried to a town in the hill country of Judea.

—Luke 1:39

Chapter Thirty Three

Mountain Woman Mary

At that time, Mary got ready and hurried to a town in the hill country of Judea.

—Luke 1:39

At first glance, the gospel writer Luke does not indicate that Mary, the mother of Jesus, was a mountain traveler. However, researchers show that some Bible translators do indicate that the "hill country of Judea" could be considered the "mountain country of Judea." Maps of this area show that some of the elevations are over 3,000 feet. We are not told about the terrain on which Mary traveled. We only know that she hurried from Nazareth to the hill country of Judea where she entered the home of her relative, Elizabeth.

In early Montana history, women in the Gallatin Canyon traveled hilly or mountainous trails to visit one another, too. Sometimes they rode horses to get to their destinations. Whenever the pioneer women in Gallatin Canyon were able to visit one another, they cherished their companionship and their conversations. No doubt some of their talk was about babies already born, babies soon-to-be born or possibly about children who died in the harsh conditions of those early settler days.

The purpose of Mary's visit to Elizabeth was to share companionship and conversation about two very special babies. Just prior to the verse which tells us about Mary getting ready and hurrying to Elizabeth's town, we read

179

that the angel Gabriel came to Mary with two amazing announcements. The first announcement is that she, Mary, a virgin, will give birth to a Son who will be Jesus, the Holy One, the Son of God, the One who will reign on the throne of David, the One whose kingdom will never end. The angel Gabriel explains to Mary that the power of the Most High would cause this baby to be conceived within her body.

The second announcement is that Mary's relative, Elizabeth, is also going to have a baby. Mary learned about Elizabeth's pregnancy from the same angel who told Mary that she, herself, would become pregnant. Elderly Elizabeth had been barren—unable to conceive and give birth to children. In Israel's culture, this would be a cause for shame. In fact, when Elizabeth became pregnant, she exclaimed,

> *The Lord has done this for me. . . in these days, he has shown*
> *his favor and taken away his disgrace among the people.*
> —Luke 1:25

The contrast between these two women is remarkable. Elizabeth was old. Mary was young. Elizabeth was married. Mary was not. Elizabeth's pregnancy would take away her disgrace. Mary's pregnancy would bring her disgrace because she was not yet married.

The similarities between Mary and Elizabeth are also noteworthy. Each is filled with the Holy Spirit. Luke 1:41 tells us, *"Elizabeth was filled with the Holy Spirit."* Luke 1:35 records that the angel promised Mary, *"The Holy Spirit will come upon you."*

The sons of these two women were also filled with the Holy Spirit. In fact, Elizabeth's baby John leaped for joy in Elizabeth's womb when Mary arrived at Elizabeth's home and greeted her. Luke 1:68-79 also affirms John's special calling as a holy prophet who prepared the way for Jesus. Mary's baby Jesus was conceived by the Holy Spirit. So the Holy Spirit's power is evident in the life of each mother and each baby in this story of miraculous births.

We are not told the entirety of what Mary and Elizabeth talked about during their weeks of fellowship. We do know that Elizabeth's husband, Zechariah, could not verbally interrupt their dialogue because he could not speak (see Luke 1:5-24). No doubt, Mary and Elizabeth shared insights about prophesy, angels, babies, and the nature of God. Elizabeth loudly proclaims both God's goodness to herself and God's immense blessing to Mary (Luke 1:42-45). Mary sings a song of praise to God for who He is, for what he has done and for what He will do (Luke 1:46-55).

Mary and Elizabeth's companionship and conversations lasted for three months. The Bible does not tell us if Mary stayed with Elizabeth long enough to witness the birth of John. However, we do know that Mary sought female friendship at the beginning of her journey as the mother of Jesus, her son and her Savior. Mary also sought female consolation at the end of her journey as the mother of Jesus who was both her son and her Savior. Thirty-three years after Jesus' birth, *"near the cross of Jesus stood his mother, his mother's sister, Mary the wife of Clopas and Mary Magdalene"* (John 19:25). That day on Mount Calvary, Mountain Woman Mary likely remembered the words of the Angel Gabriel, *"For nothing is impossible with God"* and her own words, *"I am the Lord's servant."*

In our conversations, may those be our words, as well.

Reflections: Read Luke 1:26-56

1. What do you think Mary thought about on her three to five day journey from Nazareth to Elizabeth's house? (Consider that she might have prayed "Hannah's Prayer" as recorded in I Samuel 2:1-10 as she traveled.)

2. List and reflect on God's attributes and actions as described in Mary's Song (Luke 1:46-55).

Compare these to the attributes of God in Hannah's prayer (I Samuel 2:1-10).

3. When you spend time with friends, what is the main topic of your conversations?

4. If you are able to say with Mary, *"I am the Lord's Servant":* how does your life reflect that testimony?

Jesus left there and went along the Sea of Galilee. Then he went up on a mountainside and sat down. . . . Jesus called his disciples to him.

—Matthew 15:29 and 32a

Chapter Thirty Four

Mountain Man Matthew

As Jesus went on from there, he saw a man named Matthew sitting at the tax collector's booth. "Follow me," he told him and Matthew got up and followed him.

—Matthew 9:9

Jesus left there and went along the Sea of Galilee. Then he went up on a mountainside and sat down. . . . Jesus called his disciples to him.

–Matthew 15:29 and 32a

On a sunny day in May, I took a hike on Kirk Hill near Bozeman, MT. I had just read the Gospel of Matthew and used the hiking time to meditate on this marvelous book. Kirk Hill has three loops of hiking trails with various signs designating how to complete the loops. As I came to each sign post, I thought of the phrase, "Follow Me." I reflected on how quickly Matthew "got up and followed Jesus." When I got to the top of Kirk Hill, I was surprised to see a crude framework made from fallen logs. This structure made me wonder what Matthew's tax collector's booth looked like. My contemplations continued while I walked on the highest loop of the trail. I captured a few photographic images of the Gallatin Valley and the city of Bozeman far below. I was reminded of Matthew's account of the devil taking Jesus to a high mountain and showing him the *"kingdoms of the world"* (Matthew 4:8).

185

Matthew never hiked up Kirk Hill; but Matthew knew about mountains. Matthew also knew about kingdoms of the world. Matthew lived in Capernaum, a village on the northern shore of the Sea of Galilee, with mountains nearby. Matthew, also known as Levi, was a tax collector employed by the Roman government under the authority of King Herod Antipas. This was the same Herod who was responsible for the beheading of John, the Baptist. Matthew describes John the Baptist as the preacher who said,

> *"Repent, for the Kingdom of Heaven is near."*
> —Matthew 3:2

So how did Matthew transform from being a tax collector for King Herod (in an earthly kingdom) to being a follower of King Jesus (in a heavenly Kingdom)? How did Matthew leave employment in the kingdom of this world and become a writer whose Gospel uses the word "kingdom" fifty five times? Why did Matthew, in writing about his new King, record "Kingdom of Heaven" thirty two times and "Kingdom of God" four times?

Scholars widely accept the premise that Matthew wrote his gospel for a hearing and reading audience made up primarily of Jews who were waiting for an earthly king. Matthew introduces Jesus Christ as the *"son of David"* (Matt. 1:1). The Jews of Matthew's day knew the history of David as their ancestors' king. Matthew also records that the Magi asked, *"Where is the one who has been born king of the Jews?"* (Matt. 2:2). Matthew's details about Jesus' crucifixion include, *"Above his head they placed the written charge against him: THIS IS JESUS, THE KING OF THE JEWS"* (Matt. 27:37).

So, back to the question: How did Matthew transform from being a tax collector for King Herod to being a follower of King Jesus? His calling and his response to Jesus' call seem abrupt (see Matt. 9:9). However, when we realize that Matthew collected taxes in Capernaum, we could imagine that Matthew had opportunity to hear a lot about Jesus because Jesus *"went and lived in Capernaum. . . . and began to preach, 'Repent, for the Kingdom of heaven is near'"* (Matt. 4:13, 17). Jesus preached his Sermon on the Mount near Capernaum. The first disciples whom Jesus called were fishermen in the Sea of Galilee right near Capernaum. Possibly, even before he was called to follow Jesus, Matthew had been hearing, *"Blessed are those who are persecuted because of righteousness, for theirs is the kingdom of heaven"* (Matt. 5:10). So, when Jesus called, Matthew followed.

Matthew, as a Jew, knew that the Jews were looking for an earthly king to set up an earthly kingdom. Matthew heard King Jesus teach in parables: *"the kingdom of heaven is like. . . ."* (Matthew 13). Matthew was no doubt with the other disciples when they argued about who was greatest in the kingdom of heaven (Matthew 18:1). Matthew also had another call from Jesus, *"Then the King will say. . . 'Come. . . take your inheritance, the kingdom prepared for you since the creation of the world'"* (Matthew 25:34).

Matthew followed Jesus; he experienced the Holy Spirit's power at Pentecost and wrote his gospel. Mountain Man Matthew knew that the mountain teachings of Jesus were not about the kingdoms of this world. Inspired by the Holy Spirit, Matthew knew the truth of:

> *But seek first His Kingdom and His righteousness, and all these things will be given to you as well.*
> —Matthew 6:33

Matthew wrote to his fellow Jews to teach them that the Kingdom of God is a kingdom of following Jesus; that the kingdom of God is where God now rules in grace and that the kingdom of God is where God will rule in glory for all eternity.

> *When the Son of Man comes in his glory, and all the angels with him, he will sit on his throne in the heavenly glory.*
> —Matthew 25:31

Hallelujah! Our God reigns! Matthew knew it and we can too.

Reflections: Read each of the following passages.

Reflect/discuss what might have been Matthew's response to each circumstance.

1. Matthew 9:9-13

   How did Matthew practice hospitality? Who is at his home?

   What might have been the topics of conversation?

2. Matthew 10:1-10

   How would Matthew's occupation as a tax collector influence his response to Jesus' instructions?

3. Matthew 17:24-27

   This passage speaks about a temple tax; however, do you think that Matthew might at one time have collected "fishermen" taxes from his fellow apostles?

4. Matthew 21:28-32 and Matthew 22:15-22

    Do you think Matthew "heard" these teachings differently than the other disciples?

5. Matthew 26:55-56

    Whose kingdom is Matthew following in this passage?

6. Matthew 28:16-20

    Whose kingdom is Matthew following in this passage?

7. To what kingdom do you belong?

Jesus went up on a mountainside and called to him those he wanted and they came to him.

—Mark 3:13

Chapter Thirty Five

Mountain Man Mark

Jesus went up on a mountainside and called to him those he wanted and they came to him.

—Mark 3:13

The Gospel written by mountain man Mark is full of direct action. Jesus went up a mountain. Jesus called. People came. Scholars have described this book as a narrative that has no detours and one in which the text almost runs.

When I read the book of Mark, I think about my friend Frank who is a man of action. Frank works hard at his job. To relieve stress he runs up a mountain hiking trail near Bozeman, Montana. This trail is known as the "M" because of the large white washed stones which form the letter "M" on the mountain. There are actually three trails on the "M." Frank, age 55, takes no detours as he runs up the steepest trail: 850 feet elevation gain in ¾ mile in a time of fourteen minutes. Frank runs this trail 80-100 times per year to keep in shape for elk hunting when he often has to walk a total of 20 miles to "pack out" his trophy after a successful hunt. Frank's actions have a purpose.

Mountain Man Mark, like Frank, is a man of purposeful action. As a Gospel writer, Mark is adept at describing the "who, what, when, where, why and how" of the story. He never uses his own name in this book of the Bible. However, most Biblical scholars feel that Mark describes himself in Mark 14:51-52, *"A young man, wearing nothing but a linen garment, was following Jesus. When they seized him, he fled naked, leaving his garment behind."*

Even though we do not know for certain that the young man in this passage is Mark, we do know:

> ➤ Mark's full name of John Mark represents both his Jewish and Roman heritage.
> ➤ Mark was a close friend of the Apostle Peter (see I Peter 5:13).
> ➤ Mark is generally believed to have written the Gospel of Mark as the voice of Peter.
> ➤ Mark was the son of Mary in whose home believers met to pray for Peter when he was in prison (Acts 12).
> ➤ John Mark accompanied Paul and Barnabas, his cousin, on missionary journeys (Acts 13 and 15, Col. 4:10 and II Tim. 4:11).

The "how" of Mark's gospel is that he wrote with a sense of urgency. Already in the first chapter we read, *"at once. . . at once. . . without delay. . . quickly. . . as soon as. . . immediately. . . at once. . . ."* This sets the tone for the entire Gospel which shows action with a purpose.

The "why" of Mark's Gospel is the most important. Mark states his purpose in the very first verse: *"The beginning of the gospel about Jesus Christ, the Son of God"* (Mark 1:1). Mark's purpose was to write the Good News about Jesus Christ, the Son of God.

The writer Mark, the apostle Peter, and my friend Frank are all men of action and purpose. However, each of them gives honor to the One whose action and purpose is most important of all: Jesus Christ, the Son of God. Mark shows that Jesus called and people came. The action of Jesus is action which showed authority and brought amazement.

> *The people were amazed at his teaching, because he taught as one who had authority. . . . the people were all so amazed that they asked each other, "What is this? A new teaching—and with authority!"*
>
> —Mark 1:22 and 27a

Mark presents Jesus Christ as the Son of God who climbed mountains to teach and to pray. Mark presents Jesus Christ as the Son of God who had authority. Mark gives clear evidence of Jesus' authority over demons, of Jesus' authority over disease and of Jesus' authority over nature.

Most importantly, Mark presents Jesus Christ as the eternal Son of God. The action in Jesus' life appears to stop in Mark 15:37, *"With a loud cry, Jesus breathed his last."* Without delay, Mark proves Jesus' authority over sin and death as he writes,

> *Do not be alarmed, you are looking for Jesus the Nazarene,*
> *who was crucified. He has risen!*
>
> —Mark 16:6

Mountain man Mark makes very clear that Jesus' action and purpose do not end with His death and resurrection. Very soon, Jesus says,

> *Go into all the world and preach the good news to all creation.*
>
> —Mark 16:15

At once, *"He was taken up into heaven and he sat at the right hand of God"* (Mark 16:19). From heaven, Jesus still calls with authority. People still follow and preach the Good News.

Are you amazed?

Reflections: Read the following passages from Mark and discover Jesus' authority.

1. Mark 1:21-28 and Mark 5:1-20 describe Jesus' authority over:

2. Mark 1:29-31 and 40-45 as well as Mark 5:25-34 show Jesus' authority over:

3. Mark 2:1-12 show Jesus' authority over:

4. Mark 4:35-41 and 6:45-52 describe Jesus' authority over:

5. Mark 5:21-24 and 35-43 demonstrate Jesus' authority over:

6. Over what areas of your life does Jesus have authority?

7. In what areas of your life, do you want Jesus to have more authority?

Peter said to Jesus, "Lord, it is good for us to be here. If you wish, I will put up three shelters—one for you, one for Moses and one for Elijah."

—Matthew 17:4

Chapter Thirty Six

Mountain Man Peter

After six days Jesus took with him Peter, James and John the brother of James, and led them up a high mountain by themselves. There he was transfigured before them. His face shone like the sun, and his clothes became as white as the light. Just then there appeared before them Moses and Elijah, talking with Jesus. Peter said to Jesus, "Lord, it is good for us to be here. If you wish, I will put up three shelters—one for you, one for Moses and one for Elijah."

—Matthew 17:1-4

Simon Peter had left his fishing boat and his home by the Sea of Galilee to become a mountain climber with Jesus. Moses had left his home in Midian to become a mountain climber on Mt. Sinai. Elijah had left his home in Tishbe to become a mountain climber on Mt. Carmel. Jesus had left his home in heaven to become a mountain climber on earth.

Here they were together on a high mountain: Jesus, the Son of God; Moses, the lawgiver; Elijah, the prophet; and Peter, the passionate outspoken disciple who said, *"If you wish, I will put up three shelters—one for you, one for Moses and one for Elijah."*

Peter seemed to want to capture the moment. He was witnessing the magnificent deity of Christ—the essential nature of the Kingdom Teacher who climbed a mountain as a man, but was transfigured back into His glorious splendor as God. Peter was in the presence of Moses who had seen that same splendor at the burning bush at Mt. Horeb (also called Sinai) and whose face shown with radiance as he descended Mt. Sinai after receiving the Ten Commandments. Peter was in the presence of Elijah who had been miraculously taken up to heaven in a whirlwind.

So Peter wanted to capture the moment. *"If you wish, I will put up three shelters."* We are never told what kind of shelters Peter wanted to build there on that mountaintop.

Mountain shelters in Montana can be as simple as tipis or as elaborate as a mountain lodge which I recently saw in an advertisement published by PureWest Properties. This 11,028 square foot six bedroom lodge was offered at close to ten million dollars. This "shelter" was high on a ridge and described as nearly touching the heavenly expanse of skies.

Peter surely did not have a dwelling like this in mind; but we don't know if Peter wanted to put up three tents, three clefts in rocks or even build three tabernacles as centers for worship. Peter likely knew that the Israelites had *"prepared shelters for themselves in mountain clefts, caves and strongholds"* (Judges 6:2). Peter likely knew that David wrote about God, *"in the day of trouble, he will keep me safe in his dwelling; he will hide me in the shelter of his tabernacle and set me high on a rock"* (Psalm 27:5). Peter also knew that the tabernacle built by Moses was the place where people could worship in God's presence.

Even though we don't know what Peter wanted to build, we do know that Peter wanted to stay. *"Lord, it is good for us to be here. If you wish, I will put up three shelters."* Moses could not stay. Elijah could not stay. Jesus could not stay. Peter could not stay. As Luke describes in his account of the transfiguration, *"He (Peter) did not know what he was saying"* (Luke 9:33).

Years later, Peter **did** know what he was saying when he told the transfiguration story in his own words,

> *We did not follow cleverly invented stories when we told you*
> *about the power and coming of our Lord Jesus Christ, but*

we were eyewitnesses of his majesty. For he received honor and glory from God the Father when the voice came to him from the Majestic Glory, saying, "This is my Son, whom I love; with him I am well pleased." We ourselves heard this voice that came from heaven when we were with him on the sacred mountain.

—II Peter 1:16-18

Mountain Man Peter did not build a shelter. God did. Peter now lives with Jesus, Moses and Elijah in a place much grander than a Montana Mountain Lodge. It is good for them to be there and God is well pleased!

Reflections:

1. Read Matthew 16:13-28

   What do you learn about Peter in these events before the Transfiguration?

2. Read Matthew 17:1-8

   What impresses you the most about the Transfiguration story?

3. Read Matthew 17:9-13

   What were Jesus, Peter, James and John talking about on the way down the mountain after the Transfiguration?

4. Read Luke 22:31-34 and 52-62

   What do you learn about Peter in this account? What impresses you about verse 31?

5. Read John 21:15-19

   What do these verses tell us about Peter?

6. Read II Peter 1:10-21

   What progression do you see in Peter's life?

7. Who do you say that Jesus is?

Now when he (Jesus) saw the crowds, he went up on a mountainside and sat down. His disciples came to him and he began to teach them, saying: . . . "And why do you worry about clothes? See how the lilies of the field grow."
—Matthew 5:1 and 6:28a

Chapter Thirty Seven

Mountain Man Jesus

Now when he (Jesus) saw the crowds, he went up on a mountainside and sat down. His disciples came to him and he began to teach them, saying: . . . "And why do you worry about clothes? See how the lilies of the field grow."
—Matthew 5:1 and 6:28a

Mountain wildflowers have intrigued me ever since we moved to Montana. Therefore, when I read Jesus' "Sermon on the Mount," I like to visualize that Jesus was surrounded by mountain flowers as he sat down to teach. Notice that Jesus uses "lilies of the field" as a vivid sermon illustration. In essence, Jesus said, "Don't worry. I take care of the lilies of the field. I will take care of you."

Our Creator's care for the flowers of the field is evident in a spectacular way along Montana and Wyoming's "Beartooth Highway." This scenic drive begins in a forested montane zone, gains elevation through a subalpine vegetation zone and ascends to a treeless alpine zone. Each floral landscape shows adaptation to its environment. Petite Alpine bluebells and ground-hugging forget-me-nots lace the ground on the highest elevations where the growing season is very short. Yellow glacier lilies with fragile stems show their splendor on the subalpine terrain. Brilliant Indian Paintbrushes and softly colored Wood Nymphs spread their glory on the lower elevations where the growing season is the longest.

Jesus knew all about mountain flowers. Jesus also knew all about adaptation to environment. The Apostle's Creed identifies some of the stages of Jesus' adaptation. Jesus **was *born of the virgin Mary.*** In order to live on earth, Jesus needed to clothe himself in human flesh. In order to say, "Do not worry," in a meaningful way, Jesus had to live among worriers. We get a glimpse of the heavenly splendor that Jesus left when we read about his transfiguration on a mountain. *"His face shone like the sun, and his clothes became as white as the light"* (Matthew 17:2). In contrast, his human form *"had no beauty or majesty to attract us to him"* (Isaiah 53:2b).

The Apostle's Creed continues, Jesus Christ ***suffered under Pontius Pilate, was crucified, dead and buried; he descended into hell.*** The flesh which covered Jesus was tortured. The body that Jesus took on for our sakes was crucified. That body died. That body was buried. Our Jesus, who knew the glorious splendor of heaven (which is far beyond the splendor of any mountain flowers), descended bodily into the ravages of hell. That adaptation is beyond anything we can imagine.

The third day he rose again from the dead. Mark 16:12 tells us something about Jesus' post-resurrection metamorphosis, *"Afterword, Jesus appeared in a different form to two of them while they were walking in the country."* John further describes: *"though the doors were locked, Jesus came and stood among them and said 'Peace be with you'"* (John 20:26). The same Jesus who said, *"do not worry"* on the mountainside now miraculously appears in a locked room and says, *"peace be with you."*

He ascended into heaven and is seated at the right hand of God the Father Almighty.

> *The Son is the radiance of God's glory and the exact representation of his being sustaining all things by his powerful word. After he provided purification for sins, he sat down at the right hand of the Majesty in heaven.*
> —Hebrews 1:3

Jesus took on human flesh so that he could climb a mountain to teach. Jesus regularly climbed a mountain to pray. Jesus climbed a cruel mountain to die. Jesus climbed still another mountain to ascend back to heaven. However, Jesus' story does not end there.

From there he shall come to judge the living and the dead.

> *At that time, they will see the Son of Man coming in a cloud with power and great glory.*
>
> —Luke 21:27

We don't know what his body will look like nor what his voice will sound like at His Second Coming; but those who have believed in Jesus as Savior and Lord will no doubt hear him say, *"Do not worry. Peace be with you."*

We can be assured of this because Mountain Man Jesus once said,

> *Do not let your hearts be troubled. Trust in God, trust also in me. In my Father's house are many rooms. . . . I am going there to prepare a place for you. . . .I will come back and take you to be with me that you also may be where I am.*
>
> —John 14:1-4

I'm ready for that day! Are you?

Reflections: Pray for the Holy Spirit to reveal new truths to you as you read each of the following passages and reflect on Jesus' mountain experiences.

1. Matthew 4:8-11

2. Matthew 5:1-2 and Matthew 6:25-34

3. Luke 6:12-16

4. Luke 9:28-31

5. Luke 21:37-38 and Luke 22:39-46

6. Matthew 28:16-20

. . . And if I have a faith that can move mountains, but have not love, I am nothing.

—I Corinthians 13:2b

Chapter Thirty Eight

Mountain Man Paul

. . . And if I have a faith that can move mountains, but have not love, I am nothing.

—I Corinthians 13:2b

Paul wrote these words about faith and mountains to the Corinthians at the beginning of his well-known exhortation about love. We are not very sure about Paul's mountain experiences. Paul was born as Saul in the coastal city of Tarsus which has a mountain range thirty miles to the east. Saul's dramatic conversion occurred on the road to Damascus with mountains to the west, north and south. Paul wrote this letter to inhabitants of Corinth who could have had a view of the Oneia Mountains.

In his epistles, Paul uses more references cities than to mountains. However, when Paul writes, *"if I have a faith that can move mountains,"* he seems to be referring to the words that Jesus spoke to his disciples,

> *If you have faith as small as a mustard seed, you can say to this mountain, 'move from here to there' and it will move.*
> —Matthew 17:21

> *"Have faith in God," Jesus answered. "I tell you the truth, if anyone says to this mountain, 'go and throw yourself into the sea' and does not doubt in his heart, but believes that what he says will happen, it will be done for him."*
> —Mark 11:22

When we look closely at the context of each of these instances, it is important to remember that Paul and Jesus are not focusing as much on mountains or on faith as they are on God who is the object of faith and who is the essence of Love. Paul states that without love, he and his faith are nothing. In other words, faith that moves mountains is nothing without love. Jesus emphasizes, *"have faith in God."* Faith that moves mountains must be faith in God's power to remove obstacles in life. Faith that moves mountains depends on a right relationship with God and a relationship with others that is characterized by love.

A mountain is being moved near Whitehall, Montana. The workers at Golden Sunlight Mine must have faith that they can move a mountain elevation. They use a method called drill-blast-load-haul. They use shovels and trucks to move the mountain one load at a time.

However, these mountain men are not just moving a mountain to prove that they can move a mountain. They are not proving their faith by their works. These men are miners who are moving the mountain as they mine for gold. Shovelful by shovelful, they move rock and dirt. Shovelful by shovelful, they search for the gold hidden beneath Bull Mountain.

For Paul, too, faith to move a mountain was not about moving the mountain. His faith was all about the treasure he had in Jesus as His Savior and the riches he knew because God was His loving God.

Paul wanted the Corinthians to know that treasure as well. He urged them to live a life of love because of the God who loved them. Paul passionately wants the Corinthians to have the same focus that he does. They had been "drilling and blasting" one another in an effort to prove a superiority of gifts. The Corinthians had been "loading and hauling" divisions within the church instead of working together in unity.

Paul reminds the Corinthians that even though there are different spiritual gifts, unity in the Spirit requires that they love one another. He emphatically states that love for God and love for one another are even more important than mighty faith and trusting hope.

Mountain Man Paul is so God-focused that he names God eighty one times in I Corinthians. God is both the source and object of our faith. God is both the source and object of our hope. God's character is love. Without love, we are nothing. Without God, we are nothing. The love that proceeds from God is a treasure that shines more brightly and is worth far more than any gold found in Montana's Golden Sunlight Mine.

> *And now these three remain: faith, hope and love. But the greatest of these is love.*
>
> —I Corinthians 13:13

Reflections:

1. Read I Corinthians 12. Note verses 7-11. How is faith to be used for the "common good"?

2. Read I Corinthians 13.

   Read I Corinthians 13:4-7 again and substitute "God" for the words "love" and "it."

3. Read I Corinthians 13 again. Stop at the verse or phrase that especially speaks to you.

4. What is God saying to you?

The lake of fire is the second death. If anyone's name was not found written in the book of life, he was thrown into the lake of fire.

—Revelation 20:14b and 15

Chapter Thirty Nine

Mountain Man John

*And he carried me away in the Spirit to a mountain great
and high, and showed me the Holy City, Jerusalem, coming
down out of heaven from God.*

—Revelation 21:10

The Apostle John is considered by many to be the writer of the book
of Revelation. The Apostle John and explorer John Coulter were both
experienced mountain men. Both travelled extensively with others. Both
also had experiences which were uniquely their own.

John Coulter was a frontiersman who was a member of the Lewis and
Clark Corps of Discovery expedition from 1803-1806. John, the apostle,
was a fisherman who was a member of Jesus' band in the first century A.D.

John Coulter travelled throughout Indian plains, over the Rocky Mountains
and to the Pacific Ocean during his adventures with Lewis and Clark. The
Apostle John travelled throughout the Galilean countryside, to the Mount
of Transfiguration, to Jericho, to Jerusalem and to Mount Calvary during
his adventures with Jesus Christ.

John Coulter lived, hunted, ate, rested, worked and explored with Lewis and
Clark's expedition band for almost three years. He shared the hardships of
life and the joys of exploration with this intimate group. The Apostle John
lived, fished, ate, prayed, listened, learned and travelled with Jesus and his

expedition band for approximately three years. John shared the hardships of life and the joys of discovery with the intimate group of Jesus, Peter and James as well as with the larger group of Jesus and his special twelve.

John Coulter began a personal journey after he left Lewis and Clark. He embarked on an adventure throughout what is now Yellowstone National Park. He encountered visual and auditory experiences which he had never seen or heard before. The Apostle John had a personal journey after the death, resurrection and ascension of Jesus Christ. He was sent on an adventure to the Island of Patmos. John encountered visual and auditory experiences which he had never seen or heard before.

After his personal explorations, John Coulter described what he saw and heard as hot springs, bubbling mud pots, exploding geysers and rupturing sulfurous earth. When he told of his experiences, no one believed his fantastic tales.

After his personal vision, the Apostle John described what he saw and heard as great and marvelous signs, a spring of the water of life, fiery lake of burning sulfur, brilliance like that of a precious jewel, and streets of pure gold. When he wrote of his vision, even theologians could not agree completely on what it meant.

After John Coulter died, the truth of his explorations was confirmed. The paint pots, mud pots, geysers, fumaroles which smell like sulfur, mountains, waterfalls and canyons of Yellowstone National Park have been viewed and validated by millions of people. After the Apostle John died, his gospel, his epistles and the book of Revelation have been read by millions of people.

I do not know where mountain man John Coulter stood in relationship to Jesus Christ.

I do know where mountain man John, the Apostle, stood in relationship to Jesus Christ. Listen to him:

From his gospel:

These are written that you may believe that Jesus is the Christ, the Son of God, and that by believing you may have life in his name.

—John 20:31

From his epistle:

Jesus Christ, the Righteous One. . . is the atoning sacrifice for our sins.

—I John 2:1-2

From his revelation:

The revelation of Jesus Christ, which God gave him to show his servants what must soon take place. . . . He carried me away in the Spirit to a mountain great and high. . . I, Jesus, have sent my angel to give you this testimony for the churches . . . he who testifies to these things says, "Yes, I am coming soon." Amen. Come, Lord Jesus.

—from Revelation chapters 1, 21 and 22

Amen. Come, Lord Jesus, so that we can discover, explore and enjoy You and Your new heaven and earth forever and ever.

Reflections: Read Revelation chapter 21

Compare and contrast these passages from the Gospel of John and the book of Revelation.

1. John 1:14 and Rev. 21:3

2. John 4:13-14 and Rev. 21:6

3. John 10:22-24 and Rev. 21:10

4. John 1:14 and Rev. 21:11

5. John 7:14-15; 28-29 and Rev. 21:22

6. John 8:12 and Rev. 21:23-24

7. John 1:29 and Rev. 5:6-14 and Rev. 14:1-5

8. Which comparison is the most meaningful to you?

For the LORD is the great God, the great King above all gods.
In His hand are the depths of the earth, and the mountain
peaks belong to Him.

—Psalm 95:3 and 4

Chapter Forty

Meeting God on the Mountain

> *"I watched as he opened the sixth seal. There was a great earthquake. . . . The sky receded like a scroll, rolling up, and every mountain and island was removed from its place."*
> —Revelation 6:12a and 14

Michael Snyder recently wrote that a magnitude-4.8 earthquake at Yellowstone National Park had observers very worried. For Michael Snyder, the anticipation of a massive Yellowstone earthquake brings fear because of the effect it would have on the ecosystem. After scientific study, Snyder concludes that much of the United States would be uninhabitable if there would be a massive eruption at Yellowstone.

Earthquakes are a disruption of creation. Earthquakes make us think of darkness; the earth being formless and empty. Where have we heard these words? Genesis 1:1-2 tells us,

> *In the beginning, God created the heavens and the earth. Now the earth was formless and empty, darkness was over the surface of the deep. . . .And God said, "Let there be light," and there was light.*

In the beginning, God created the heavens and the earth. God then created mankind to have a relationship with Him. Sin disrupted that relationship. Sin brought new chaos not only to God's relationship with mankind, but also to God's relationship with nature. However, God's control over man and God's control over nature were not destroyed.

Snyder's fear of the devastation of earthquakes reminded me of Jeremiah's lament,

> *I looked at the earth, and it was formless and empty and at the heavens and their light was gone. I looked at the mountains and they were quaking; all the hills were swaying.*
> —Jeremiah 4:23 and 24

In the Old Testament, Mountain Man Jeremiah shows that he recognizes the quaking mountains are under the control of his God when he calls out, *"Ah, Sovereign LORD"* (Jer. 4: 10). Jeremiah knew that when the earth was formless and void, his Sovereign LORD spoke and there was light. Jeremiah knew that when the mountains quake, his Sovereign LORD is revealing His presence and His power. Jeremiah experienced disruptive events in nature; however, Jeremiah did not focus only on the event itself. Jeremiah focused on the Creator God who orchestrated these events to draw him closer into relationship with his God. His God of the mountains could reverse nature to have His way.

In the New Testament, Mary Magdalene experienced God's control over chaos in her life when Jesus cast out seven demons (Luke 8:2). Mary Magdalene experienced a new relationship with God after having lived in darkness. Mary Magdalene also saw God's control over nature. She felt the earth shake and the rocks split when Jesus died (Matthew 27). A short time later, Mary Magdalene saw the effects of a *"violent earthquake"* when Jesus arose from the dead (Matthew 28). She talked with her risen *"Rabboni"* and testified *"I have seen the* **Lord** *"* (John 20:18). Mary Magdalene recognized that God could reverse her life and could reverse nature to have His way.

In the final book of the New Testament, the Apostle John is given a vision of the reversal of the "in the beginning" creation:

There was a great earthquake. The sun turned black like sackcloth. . . . The sky receded like a scroll, rolling up and every mountain and island was removed from its place.
—Rev. 6:14

Then I saw a new heaven and a new earth, for the first heaven and the first earth had passed away.
—Rev. 21:1

The city does not need the sun or the moon to shine on it, for the glory of God gives it light and the Lamb is its light.
—Rev. 21:23

The God of the mountains gave John a revelation about judgment at the end of time when an earthquake to end all earthquakes will usher in a new creation with no more chaos and no more darkness. John saw a future when there will be complete restoration of relationship between God and nature as well as complete restoration between God and those who believe in the Lamb of God who takes away the darkness of the world.

Psalm 46:1-3 and 10-11 give this testimony about our God of the Mountains:

God is our refuge and our strength, an ever present help in trouble. Therefore, we will not fear though the earth give way and the mountains fall into the heart of the sea, though its water roar and foam and the mountains quake with their surging. . . . .

"Be still and know that I am God: I will be exalted among the nations, I will be exalted in the earth." . . . The LORD Almighty is with us; The God of Jacob is our fortress. Selah

Michael Snyder asserted that a large earthquake at Yellowstone would bring the United States to its knees. Centuries earlier, the Apostle Paul wrote to the Romans:

> *For we shall all stand before God's judgment. It is written: . . .*
> *'every knee will bow before me.'*
>
> —Romans 14:10-11

The God of the mountains has the final say. His Presence and Power will accomplish His will. The mountain peaks belong to Him. In the end, it might even take a quaking removal of mountains to show the world that God is the Sovereign LORD over all creation. Be still and know that He is God!

Mountain men and women who meet God on the mountain bow their knees before Him.

How about you?

Reflections: Pray for the Holy Spirit's guidance as you read each of the following passages and reflect on what it says about the God of the mountains.

1. Isaiah 54:10

2. Ezekiel 38:19-23

3. Nahum 1:1-7

4. Zechariah 14:3-9

5. II Peter 3:10-18

6. Revelation 16:15-21

7. Revelation 20:11 through Revelation 21:5

Works Consulted

Chapter 2: Mountain Man Noah

Kline, Meredith G, *New Bible Commentary: Revised, Genesis* (Grand Rapids: Eerdmans, 1970), 88-89.

www.noahsarksearch.com/

Chapter 3: Mountain Man Abraham

Boice, James Montgomery, *Genesis: Volume 2, A New Beginning, Genesis 12-36* (Grand Rapids: Baker Book House, 1998), 682-708.

Chapter 4: Mountain Man Moses

Keil, C.F., D.D. and F. Delitzsch, D.D., *Biblical Commentary on the Old Testament, Pentateuch, Vol.3.* (Grand Rapids: Eerdmans, 1951), 88-105.

Chapter 5: Mountain Man Aaron

Philip, James, *Mastering the Old Testament Vol. 4, Numbers* (Dallas: Word Inc., 1987), 228-229.

Chapter 6: Mountain Man Joshua

Hess, Richard S., *Tyndale Old Testament Commentaries: Vol. 6, Joshua* (Downers Grove: Inter-Varsity Press, 1996), 171-174.

Huffman, John, *Mastering the Old Testament: Vol. 6 Joshua* (Dallas: Word Inc., 1986), 145-146.

Tenney, Merrill C., *Zondervan Pictorial Encyclopedia of the Bible: Vol. 5 Q-Z.* (Grand Rapids: Zondervan, 1976), 205-208.

Woudstra, Marten H., *New International Commentary of the Old Testament: Joshua* (Grand Rapids: Eerdmans, 1981), 148-150.

Chapter 7: Mountain Woman Deborah

Allsop, Pam, interview on 08.25.2011 in Bozeman, Montana.

Tenney, Merrill C., *Zondervan Pictorial Encyclopedia of the Bible: Vol. 3 H-L* (Grand Rapids: Zondervan, 1976), 829-830.

Tenney, Merrill C., *Zondervan Pictorial Encyclopedia of the Bible: Vol. 5 Q-Z* (Grand Rapids: Zondervan, 1976), 302.

www.Montanaoutfitters.org

Chapter 8: Mountain Man Jonathan

Chafin, Kenneth, *Mastering the Old Testament: Volume 8: 1 and 2 Samuel* (Dallas: Word, 1998), 103-131.

Keil, C.F., D.D. and F. Delitzsch, D.D., *Biblical Commentary on the Old Testament, Books of Samuel* (Grand Rapids: Eerdmans, 1950), 135-148.

Tenney, Merrill C., *Zondervan Pictorial Encyclopedia of the Bible: Vol. 3 H- L* (Grand Rapids: Zondervan, 1976), 679-681.

www.bibleplaces.com/michmash/

http://en.wikipedia.org/wiki/Rock_climbing

Chapter 9: Mountain Man Saul

Keil, C.F., D.D. and F. Delitzsch, D.D., *Biblical Commentary on the Old Testament: The Books of Samuel* (Grand Rapid: Eerdmans, 1950), 228-233.

Tenney, Merrill C., *Zondervan Pictorial Encyclopedia of the Bible: Vol. 5 Q-Z* (Grand Rapids: Zondervan, 1976), 286-290.

www.pbs.org/lewisandclark/

Chapter 10: Mountain Woman Abigail

Harris, Rev. W. Harris, *The Preacher's Complete Homiletic Commentary on the First and Second Books of Samuel* (Grand Rapids: Baker Books, 1996), 243-250.

http://start.start.cortera.com/company/research/k9l2tr6j/rocky-mountain-hospitality/

Tenney, Merrill C., *Zondervan Pictorial Encyclopedia of the Bible: Vol. 1 A-C* (Grand Rapids: Zondervan, 1976), 12.

Chapter 11: Mountain Man David

Bos, Rev. Mary, *Loss and Grief Class: Parish Nursing*. Calvin College: Department of Nursing, Grand Rapids, 2006.

Tenney, Merrill C., *Zondervan Pictorial Encyclopedia of the Bible: Vol. 4 M-P* (Grand Rapids: Zondervan, 1975, 1976), 299-302.

Chapter 12: Mountain Man Isaiah (part 1)

McKenna, David, *Mastering the Old Testament: Vol. 16b Isaiah 40-66* (Dallas: Word, 1994), 405-420

Oswalt, John N, *Book of Isaiah Chapters 40-66* (Grand Rapids: Eerdmans, 1998), 43-75.

Tenney, Merrill C., *Zondervan Pictorial Encyclopedia of the Bible: Vol. 3 H-L* (Grand Rapids: Zondervan, 1976), 313-331 and 459-494.

www.emagazine.com/dailynews /shouting-from-the-mountaintop/ August 8, 2010.

Chapter 13: Mountain Man Isaiah (part 2)

Babcock, Maltbie, *This is My Father's World* Text, 1901.

Keil, C.F., D.D. and F. Delitzsch, D.D., Biblical Commentary on the Old Testament: Isaiah Vol. 2 (Grand Rapids: Eerdmans, 1954), 256-268 and 353-360.

McKenna, David, *Mastering the Old Testament: Vol. 16b Isaiah 40-66* (Dallas: Word, 1994), 503-517 and 538-562.

Oswalt, John N, *Book of Isaiah Chapters 40-66* (Grand Rapids: Eerdmans, 1998), 285-300 and 432-438.

Tenney, Merrill C., *Zondervan Pictorial Encyclopedia of the Bible: Vol. 3 H-L* (Grand Rapids: Zondervan, 1976), 313-331.

Chapter 14: Mountain Man Elijah

Didley, Russell, *Mastering the Old Testament, Volume 9: 1, 2 Kings* (Dallas: Word, 1987), 209-215.

Tenney, Merrill C., *Zondervan Pictorial Encyclopedia of the Bible: Vol. 2. D-G* (Grand Rapids: Zondervan, 1976),284-286.

Chapter 15: Mountain Man Elisha

Dilday, Russell, *Mastering the Old Testament, Volume 9: 1 and 2 Kings* (Dallas: Word, 1987).

Keil, C.F., D.D. and F. Delitzsch, D.D., *Biblical Commentary on the Old Testament, Kings* (Grand Rapids: Eerdmans, 1950).

Tenney, Merrill C., *Zondervan Pictorial Encyclopedia of the Bible: Vol. 1 A-C* (Grand Rapids: Zondervan, 1976).

Chapter 16: Mountain Man Solomon (part 1)

Tenney, Merrill C., *Zondervan Pictorial Encyclopedia of the Bible, Vol. 5 Q-Z* (Grand Rapids: Zondervan, 1976), 469-477 and 622-634.

Wolfendale, R.E. James, *The Preacher's Complete Homiletic Commentary: 1&11 Chronicles* (Grand Rapids: Baker Books, 1996), 150-154.

http://stonecutterblogspot.com/2011/04/lsot-trade-of-stone-cutting.html

Chapter 17: Mountain Man Solomon (part 2)

Tenney, Merrill C., *Zondervan Pictorial Encyclopedia of the Bible, Vol. 5. Q-Z* (Grand Rapids: Zondervan, 1976), 469-479.

http://goldwest.visitmt.com/communities/wisdom.htm

Chapter 18: Mountain Man Hezekiah

Allen, Leslie, *Mastering the Old Testament: Volume 10 1, 2 Chronicles* (Dallas: Word, 1987).

McKenna, David, *Mastering the Old Testament: Volume 16a, Isaiah 1-39* (Dallas: Word, 1994).

www.NationalDayofPrayer.org.

Chapter 19: Mountain Man Nehemiah

Fensham, F. Charles, *International Commentary on the Old Testament: The Book of Ezra, Nehemiah* (Grand Rapids: Eerdmans, 1982), 1-27 and 221-234.

Tenney, Merrill C., *Zondervan Pictorial Encyclopedia of the Bible: Vol.4 M-P* (Grand Rapids: Zondervan, 1975, 1976), 404-407.

http://onefortheroad1187.blogspot.com/2005/06/soldiers-chapel.html

http://www.lonepeaklookout.com/news/article

Chapter 20: Mountain Man Job (part 1)

Barnes, Albert, *Notes on the Old Testament: Job* (Grand Rapids: Baker reprinted from the 1847 edition published by Blackie and Son, London), 59-73.

Hartley, John E., *New International Commentary on the Old Testament: the Book of Job* (Grand Rapids: Eerdmans, 1988), 373-384.

www.Lifeandland.org/2009/02/job-in-the-land-of-uz

Chapter 21: Mountain Man Job (part 2)

McKenna, David, *Mastering the Old Testament: Volume 12 Job* (Dallas: Word, 1986).

http://www.angelfire.com/punk2/walktheplank/mountgoats.html

http://www.crownofthecontinent.net/content/goat-lick-crossing-on-highway2/cotCFDAECE4F2E71943D

Chapter 22: Mountain Woman: the Shunnamite

Keil, C.F., D.D. and F. Delitzsch, D.D., *Biblical Commentary on the Old Testament: Kings* (Grand Rapids: Eerdmans, 1950), 310-314.

Lockyer, Herbert, *Women of the Bible* (Grand Rapids: Zondervan, 1967), 205-210.

Small, Lawrence F., ed., *Religion in Montana: Pathways to the Present Vol. I* (Billings: Rocky Mountain College with Helena: Falcon Press, 1992), 106-114.

Chapter 23: Mountain Man Asa

Barker, Rocky, *Scorched Earth: How the fires of Yellowstone changed America* (Washington: Island Press, 2005).

Boice, James Montgomery, *Psalms: Volume 2, Psalms 42-106* (Grand Rapids: Baker, 1998), 680-686.

Simpson, Ross, *The Fires of '88: Yellowstone Park and Montana in Flames* (Helena: American Geographic Publishing, 1989).

Weisel, Artur, *Old Testament Library: the Psalms* (Philadelphia: Westminster Press, 1962), 561-564.

Williams, Donald, *Mastering the Old Testament: Psalms 73-150* (Dallas: Word, 1987), 101-107.

Chapter 24: Mountain Man Jeremiah

Brueggeman, Walter, *A Commentary on Jeremiah* (Grand Rapids: Eerdmans, 1998), 424-437.

Gouras, Matt, *"1980's Big Sky 'mountain man' abductor seeks parole"* (Bozeman Daily Chronicle: Bozeman, MT, 15 April, 2012 A1 +5).

Keil, C.F., D.D. and F. Delitzsch, D.D., *Biblical Commentary on the Old Testament: Jeremiah, Volume 2.* (Grand Rapids: Eerdmans, 1950), 177-197.

Tenney, Merrill C., *Zondervan Pictorial Encyclopedia of the Bible: Volume 1 A-C* (Grand Rapids: Zondervan, 1975), 755.

Tenney, Merrill C., *Zondervan Pictorial Encyclopedia of the Bible: Volume 4 M-P* (Grand Rapids: Zondervan, 1975, 1976), 302.

Thompson, J.A., *Book of Jeremiah* (Grand Rapids: Eerdmans, 1980), 3-124 and 685-694.

Chapter 25: Mountain Man Ezekiel

Keil, C.F., D.D. and F. Delitzsch, D.D, *Biblical Commentary on the Old Testament: Ezekiel, Vol. 11* (Grand Rapids: Eerdmans, 1950).

Lutey, Tom, *Lambs move to pasture on Montana ranch* (Bozeman Daily Chronicle Bozeman, MT 25 May, 2012 Section C 4).

Wright, Christopher J.H., *Message of Ezekiel* (Dover's Grove: Inter-Varsity Press, 2001), 273-283.

www.bairfamilymuseum.org

Interview with Sid and Ethel Dykstra in Bozeman, MT on June 9, 2012.

Chapter 26 Mountain Man Daniel

Keil, C.F., D.D. and F. Delitzsch, D.D., *Biblical Commentary on the Old Testament, Daniel* (Grand Rapids: Eerdmans, 1949), 84-114.

Tenney, Merrill C., *Zondervan Pictorial Encyclopedia of the Bible, Vol. 2 D-G* (Grand Rapids: Zondervan, 1976), 12-23.

The Geologic Story of Yellowstone National Park (Geologic Survey Bulletin #1347, reprinted by Yellowstone Library and Museum Association in cooperation with US Geologic Survey, 1976).

Chapter 27: Mountain Man Joel

Boice, James Montgomery, *Minor Prophets, Volume 1 Hosea-Jonah* (Grand Rapids: Baker, 1983), 119-156.

Keil, C.F., D.D. and F. Delitzsch, D.D., *Biblical Commentary on the Old Testament, Minor Prophet Volume 1* (Grand Rapids: Eerdmans, 1954), 169-232.

Oglivie, Lloyd J., *Mastering the Old Testament, Hosea-Jonah* (Dallas: Word, 1990), 205-225.

Chapter 28: Mountain Man Amos

Boice, James Montgomery, *Minor Prophets Volume 1 Hosea-Jonah* (Grand Rapids: Baker, 1983), 161-231.

Brown, F., S. Driver and C. Briggs, *Brown-Driver-Briggs Hebrew and English Lexicon* (Peabody, Mass: Hendrickson, 1996), 838-839.

Oglivie, Lloyd J., *Mastering the Old Testament Hosea-Jonah* (Dallas: Word 1990), 268-364.

Spangler, Ann, *Names of God* (Grand Rapids: Zondervan, 2004), 40-50.

https://en.wikipedia.org/wiki/Mount_Sentinel

Chapter 29: Mountain Man Obadiah

Keil, C.F., D.D. and F. Delitzsch, D.D., *Biblical Commentary on the Old Testament Minor Prophets Volume 1* (Grand Rapids: Eerdmans, 1954), 335-378.

LaTray, Danette, *Granite begins with Silver* (Philipsburg Mail Publication, June 3, 1980, Reprinted in Discover 1, 2011), 34.

Oglivie, Lloyd J, *Mastering the Old Testament Hosea-Jonah* (Dallas: Word, 1990), 368-382.

http://www.growingchristians.org/dfgc/pride.htm

Chapter 30: Mountain Man Micah

Keil, C.F., D.D. and F. Delitzsch, D.D., *Biblical Commentary on the Old Testament Minor Prophets Volume 1* (Grand Rapids: Eerdmans, 1954), 419-515.

Kaiser, Walter, *Mastering the Old Testament Volume 2 Micah, Nahum, Habakkuk, Zephaniah, Haggai, Zechariah, Malachi* (Dallas: Word, 1992). 21-94.

http://www.juliaspriggs.com/Pages/Micah.aspx.

Chapter 31: Mountain Man Habakkuk

Hill, Andrew E. and John H. Walton, *Survey of the Old Testament* (Grand Rapids: Zondervan, 1991) 400-405.

Kaiser, Walter, *Mastering the Old Testament Volume 2: Micah, Nahum, Habakkuk Zephaniah, Haggai, Zechariah, Malachi* (Dallas: Word, 1992), 141-203.

http://en.wikipedia.org/wiki/Avalanche_transceiver

http://science.howstuffworks.com/nature/natural-disasters/avanche2.htm

Chapter 32: Mountain Man Haggai

Hill, Andrew E. and John H. Walton, *Survey of the Old Testament* (Grand Rapids: Zondervan, 1991), 410-415.

Kaiser, Walter, *Mastering the Old Testament, Volume 21: Micah, Nahum, Habakkuk, Zephaniah, Haggai, Zechariah, Malachi* (Dallas: Word, 1992), 241-282.

Tenney, Merrill C., *Zondervan Pictorial Encyclopedia of the Bible, Vol. 3 H-L* (Grand Rapids: Zondervan, 1976), 11-14.

http://www.virginiacitymt.com/Nevada.asp

Chapter 33: Mountain Woman Mary

Cronin, Janet and Dorothy Vick, *Montana's Gallatin Canyon* (Missoula: Mountain Press, 1992), 87-112.

Larson, Bruce, *Mastering the New Testament, Vol. 3. Luke* (Dallas: Word, 1983), 31-40.

Tenney, Merrill C., *Zondervan Pictorial Encyclopedia of the Bible, Vol.4 M-P* (Grand Rapids: Zondervan 1975, 1976), 106-112.

www.Biblos.com translations of the Gospel of Luke.

Chapter 34: Mountain Man Matthew

Ausburger, Myron S, *Mastering the New Testament: Matthew* (Word, Inc. 1982), 1-333.

Hendricksen, William, *New Testament Commentary: Matthew* (Grand Rapids: Baker, 1975), 1-99, 257-318, 421-442.

Knight, George W., *Holy Land* (Ohio: Barbour, 2011), 250-252.

Tenney, Merrill C., *Zondervan Pictorial Encyclopedia of the Bible, Vol. 1 A-C* (Grand Rapids: Zondervan 1975), 746-748.

Tenney, Merrill C., *Zondervan Pictorial Encyclopedia of the Bible, Vol. 3 H-L* (Grand Rapids: Zondervan 1976), 801-809.

Tenney, Merrill C., *Zondervan Pictorial Encyclopedia of the Bible, Vol. 4 M-P* (Grand Rapids: Zondervan, 1975, 1976), 120-141.

Chapter 35: Mountain Man Mark

McKenna, David, *Mastering the New Testament Volume 2 Mark* (Dallas: Word, 1982), 15-19 and 25-55.

Tenney, Merrill C., Zondervan Pictorial Encyclopedia of the Bible, *Vol.4. M-P* (Grand Rapids: Zondervan, 1975, 1976), 74-89.

Interview with Frank James in Bozeman, MT on June 21, 2013.

Chapter 36: Mountain Man Peter

Ausburger, Myron S., *Mastering the New Testament: Matthew* (Word, Inc. 1982), pp. 207-209.

Larson, Bruce, *Mastering the New Testament, Volume 3, Luke* (Dallas: Word, Inc., 1983), 172-175.

McKenna, David, *Mastering the New Testament, Volume 2, Mark.* (Dallas: Word, Inc., 1982), 182-191.

Tenney, Merrill C., *Zondervan Pictorial Encyclopedia of the Bible, Vol.4, M-P* (Grand Rapids: Zondervan, 1975, 1976), 733-739.

Tenney, Merrill C., *Zondervan Pictorial Encyclopedia of the Bible, Vol. 5, Q-Z* (Grand Rapids: Zondervan, 1976), 572-583 and 796-797.

www.purewestproperties.com MLS # 184034

Chapter 37: Mountain Man Jesus

Psalter Hymnal Grand Rapids, MI: CRC Publications, 1987, 813.

Schiemann, Donald Anthony, *Wildflowers of Montana* (Missoula Montana: Mountain Press Publishing, 2005), 1-2, 52-53, 56-57, 90-93, 120-121,134-135.

Chapter 38: Mountain Man Paul

Morris, Leon, *Tyndale New Testament Commentaries: I Corinthians* (Grand Rapids: Eerdmans, 1958), 960-974.

Tenney, Merrill C., *Zondervan Pictorial Encyclopedia of the Bible, Vol. 1 A-C* (Grand Rapids: Zondervan, 1975).

Tenney, Merrill C., Zondervan Pictorial Encyclopedia of the Bible, Vol. 2 D-G (Grand Rapids: Zondervan, 1976), 7-8 and 479-489.

Tenney, Merrill C., Zondervan Pictorial Encyclopedia of the Bible, Vol. 4 M-P (Grand Rapids: Zondervan, 1975,1976), 623-657.

Tenney, Merrill C, Zondervan Pictorial Encyclopedia of the Bible, Vol. 5 Q-Z (Grand Rapids: Zondervan, 1976), 598-602.

http://www.infomine.com/minesite/minesite.asp?site=goldensunlight.

Chapter 39: Mountain Man John

Haines, Aubrey L., *Yellowstone Story* (Niwot, Colorado: Univ. Press of Colorado, 1996), 36-38.

Hendricksen, William, *More than Conquerors: an interpretation of the book of Revelation* (Grand Rapids: Baker, 1967), 11-64 and 221-250.

http://www.pbs.org/wnet/nature/episodes/christmas-in-yellowstone/who-was- john-colter/4

Tenney, Merrill C., Zondervan Pictorial Encyclopedia of the Bible, Vol. 3. H-L (Grand Rapids: Zondervan, 1975), 637-641.

Tenney, Merrill C., *Zondervan Pictorial Encyclopedia of the Bible, Vol. 5. Q-Z* (Grand Rapids: Zondervan, 1976), 86-99.

Chapter 40: Meeting God on the Mountain

Hendricksen, William, *More than Conquerors: an interpretation of the book of Revelation* (Grand Rapids: Baker, 1967).

Ladd, George Eldon, *Commentary on the Revelation of John* (Grand Rapids: Eerdmans, 1972).

Snyder, Michael, <u>The Truth Wins</u>, April 1, 2014 sited under "What would an Eruption of the Yellowstone Supervolcano Look Like?" www.infowars.com

Printed in the United States
By Bookmasters